Uncovering Chinese Mythology

A Beginner's Guide Into the World of Chinese Myths, Enchanting Tales, Folklore, Legendary Heroes, Gods, Divine Beings, and Mythical Creatures

Lucas Russo

Table of Contents

Introduction

Chinese civilization is widely renowned for its refinement and antiquity—however, a little less is known about its mythology and folklore. The systems of beliefs traditionally associated with China—such as the teachings of Confucius (ca. 551–479 B.C.E.) or the precepts of Taoism, usually don't seem to leave space for gods, goddesses, and supernatural creatures. But this is, of course, a misconception. The mythological tradition of China is rich and unique, and the contents of many stories and fables might surprise you.

It is also, of course, a tradition that spans thousands of years, from the times of legendary emperors of over 2500 B.C.E. to modern day. In this book, I will tell you stories that were written down at various points in Chinese history and that treat about gods, emperors, nobility, and common folk. We will delve into the world of one of the most iconic Chinese creatures— Chinese dragons—as well as lesser-known ones, such as "Chinese vampires" and spirits living in trees. We will learn about deities that are believed to have all originated in one god—the God of Heaven. And finally, we will read stories of legendary emperors and of common people who encountered supernatural beings.

Let us then begin the journey from the creation of the universe to monsters and spirits that roam even the modern world. In the next chapter, we will learn a bit more about the Chinese folk religion and its influence on the mythology—before delving into the mythology itself.

Chapter 1:

Sources of the Myths

Chinese Folk Religion—a Belief Fit for Everything

Chinese folk religion, also known as Chinese popular religion, is more of an umbrella term for a set of varying beliefs than an institutionalized religion with a clear set of rules. It can combine three of the most popular Chinese traditions—Buddhism, Taoism, and Confucianism—and it adds its own beliefs to the mix, too. There are only a handful of general beliefs and precepts that govern the Chinese folk religion—and that, as we will see in the following chapters, influence Chinese mythology. Most commonly quoted, those rules include: a belief in the *shen*, or, deities and supernatural beings; a belief in the spirits of the ancestors; a view that nature is rational and the universe is balanced; and a belief that both humans and supernatural beings can affect reality (Teiser, 1995).

But what does it really mean? The balance in the universe that the Chinese folk religion promotes is often associated with the well-known (but often misunderstood) concept of Yin and Yang, the opposing, yet interconnected forces of activity and passivity, which can be observed in various forms in nature (e.g., as a duality between light and darkness or differing seasons of summer and winter). This belief will find its way to Chinese cosmogony, or the history of creation—of which we'll talk in the next chapter.

The belief in the presence of spirits and ancestors leads many followers of the Chinese folk religion to animism—a belief that places, objects, and creatures have a unique spiritual essence (Lang, 2011). This, in turn, results in the belief of countless different spirits and supernatural creatures. Traditionally, each community would have their own set of spirits and lore connected to their local creatures and ancestors whose presence could still be felt—and so, being a believer of the folk religion would be less about believing in a set of rules and more about belonging to a place with its own spiritual character. As a result, Chinese folk religion doesn't put pressure on anyone to convert to it or to participate in its rituals.

Taoism, Confucianism, and Buddhism

The three most popular religious and/or philosophical traditions of China influenced Chinese folk religion to a various extent. Taoism, a tradition that originated between the 6th and 4th century B.C.E., compiles a number of precepts that are less about belief, and more about a way of one's life—with the practice of meditation and practicing virtues such as spontaneity and wisdom (Slingerland, 2003). Followers of Dao, literally meaning "the way," believe in an element of unity that underlies all universe and from which the universe was created—a monistic view which, as we will see later, influences the folk religion's belief in the gods and goddesses all being created from one deity.

Confucianism, originating in the 6th century B.C.E. from the Chinese philosopher Confucius, shares some principles with Taoism, in that it holds a monistic belief in the God of Heaven, who is unified with an individual believing in him (Adler, 2020). Similarly, it states that the universe is in a state of perpetual creation, ordering itself according to the principles of Yin and Yang. A truly virtuous life would be to find a middle way between those polar opposites, achieving balance. Additionally, the monistic belief in the unity between Heaven and the creation promotes compassion in the followers of Confucianism—realizing the lack of boundaries between us and the other people is a perfect way of achieving said compassion. We will find the spirit of those principles at every step of the way through our journey of Chinese myth and folklore.

And finally, Buddhism, imported to China from India during the Han Dynasty (202 B.C.E.–220 C.E.), with its philosophy of achieving enlightenment through moderation, nonviolence and virtue, fit perfectly in the Chinese cultural, philosophical, and cultural landscape. As we will see in the chapter on the gods and goddesses, some of the deities, most commonly Buddhas (the ones who achieved spiritual awakening) have found their way to the Chinese pantheon.

Brief Timeline of Chinese Civilization

Before we dive into the rich world of Chinese mythology, it's worth considering a brief timeline of Chinese civilization, with the special mention of when various sources for what we know about Chinese myth originated.

Xia Dynasty (2070–1600 B.C.E.)

Although the prehistory of China reaches way back into neolithic times, the first documented Chinese dynasty—and the first period of time to be classified as ancient China—was the Xia Dynasty. It's regarded as partly mythological (Lee, 2002). It was believed to have been established by Yu the Great, a descendant of legendary emperors who will warrant a space in Chapter 5 of our book.

Shang Dynasty (1600–1046 B.C.E.)

The Shang Dynasty was concentrated in the Yellow River valley, and like in the Xia Dynasty, historical events that happened during that era are uncertain. However, some findings from the late Shang Dynasty—namely, bone inscriptions—have revealed the earliest mentions of some names appearing in Chinese myths (Birrell, 1999).

Zhou Dynasty (1046–256 B.C.E.)

The longest-ruling dynasty in the history of China, the Zhou Dynasty saw the centralization of power and an expansion in the Yellow River region—until the latter part of the period, also known as the Warring States Period, when several smaller states emerged in a political rivalry. This part of the Zhou Dynasty is also marked by momentous developments of Taoism and Confucianism. Some first, brief mythological narratives were written during that period: Much information can be parsed out from poetry dating to that era.

Qin Dynasty (221–206 B.C.E.)

The Qin Dynasty marks the first time period that could be classified as Imperial China. The dynasty managed to solidify power in the region, ensuring China's future as a superpower. To achieve that, the new emperors had to emphasize the mythical source of their power—narratives about the legendary roots of their rule come mostly from that period. The Qin Dynasty also saw some major cultural achievements: the famous Terracotta Army of the emperor Qin Shi Huang (259–210 B.C.E.) comes from that time. However, the same emperor also purportedly ordered the burning of books and the execution of many Confucian scholars, in order to eliminate intellectual diversity (Twitchett & Fairbank, 1978). Many important texts might have been lost at that time.

The Chinese Empire during the Qin Dynasty expanded and underwent a major increase in construction projects as well as cultural and administrative reforms, including the reform of the writing system. The first version of the famous Great Wall of China was built at that time. However, all that came at the cost of involuntary conscriptions of commoners into servitude so that they could work on the construction sites.

Han Dynasty (206 B.C.E.–220 C.E.)

The Han Dynasty is widely regarded as a golden period in Chinese imperial history. It established the Chinese presence in East Asia as well as expanded it westward; it created a shape of the empire that wouldn't change for centuries to come. In terms of culture and mythology, the Han Dynasty saw a major uptake in literary creation, and many compilations of poems and stories were written during that time—among them, *Shuo Yuan*, or *The Garden of Stories*, a collection of tales compiled by the scholar Liu Xiang (77–6 B.C.E.). The imperial library was also established as well as a school curriculum of philosophical and historical texts necessary for the education of scholars. Religious rituals were perfected, and the emperor was treated as the highest priest who could commune with the *shen*.

Also during this time, major technological advancements of the Chinese civilization were achieved—for example, paper was first created and used—an invention that would come to Europe only centuries later. The Great Wall of China was repaired and expanded. China also opened up for trade and cultural exchange with the West through the establishment of the Silk Road—a trade route which connected Asia and Europe.

The end of the Han Dynasty saw some unrest. A brief usurpation of power by the Xin Dynasty and the subsequent reinstatement of the Han meant a decline of the imperial might. In the end, a growing rivalry between various clans and warlords brought the end of the Han.

Six Dynasties (220–589)

The end of the Han Dynasty started an era of general unrest and quickly changing political power. For the reason of the quick succession of regimes, this period was collectively given a name of the Six Dynasties.

Even though China wasn't consolidated, trade of goods and ideas flowed freely. It was at that time when Buddhism was first introduced to China.

Sui Dynasty (581–618)

The Sui Dynasty, although short-lived, marked a crucial moment in Chinese history. It ended the era of political fracture and saw major administrative reforms, such as the minting of universal currency. Starting from this period and continuing through a number of succeeding dynasties, the most important Chinese mythological texts would be written down and compiled.

Tang Dynasty (618–907)

Another golden era of Chinese history, the Tang Dynasty was a time of technological advancement and cultural development, marking China's cultural hegemony and vast influence in the Eastern Asian region. It was the first period when three religious-philosophical traditions—Confucianism, Taoism, and Buddhism—coexisted, with Buddhism being the most popular among the common folk. Chinese poetry was perfected and prolific, and a new genre of prose developed that would give rise to the classic Chinese novel.

Cultural exchange with other countries occurred via trade, and foreign merchants were encouraged to settle in China, which created an atmosphere of multiculturalism. Cities bloomed, especially the capital of the time, Chang'an (modern-day Xi'an), which, reaching over a million inhabitants, became the largest city of the world at that time (Modelski, 2000).

Thanks to the cultural exchange and diversity of population, Chinese geography bloomed during the Tang Dynasty. Descriptions of the Silk Road and the peoples living around it, reaching as far west as medieval Iran, were written down during that time. An importation of new ideas occurred: From Persia, Christians and Zoroastrians came and formed their communities in Chinese cities.

The end of the Tang Dynasty was, yet again, marked by the rise of power of local warlords and by rebellions. Many of them were especially long-lasting and bloody, and ended with massacres of entire populations, including the foreign merchants. Following the rebellions were usurpations, which divided China.

Five Dynasties and Ten Kingdoms (907–960)

As the name suggests, this period was marked by a very quick succession of political regimes and by administrative instability. It ended with a coup which established a much more stable Song Dynasty.

Song Dynasty (960–1279)

The Song Dynasty saw a number of further technological and cultural developments in the Chinese empire. Among some of the inventions were: the first use of banknotes, the invention of gunpowder, the establishment of the imperial navy, and the invention of woodblock printing. According to calculations, the gross domestic product (GDP) of China in the 12th century was three times bigger than that of the entirety of Europe at the time (Liu, 2015). Needless to say, the Chinese population doubled, reaching 100 million (Ebrey & Walthall, 2014). This paved the way for an economical revolution, and the organization of the Chinese state saw the level of sophistication not seen anywhere in the world before.

In terms of literature, the Song Dynasty is invaluable as the source of mythology. Long and detailed accounts of mythological tales as well as transcriptions of the earlier sources meant preservation of many stories that would have been lost to time (Birrell, 1999). One of the invaluable sources for Chinese mythology coming from that time is *Taiping Yulan*, an encyclopedia containing many entries about gods and supernatural beings.

Revolution was happening not only in terms of economy but also thought. During the Song Dynasty, the teachings of Confucianism were merged and interspersed with Buddhist precepts, forming Neo-Confucianism.

Unfortunately, the Chinese era of prosperity ended with the Mongol conquest in the 13th century. Even though the advance of the Mongols was delayed for decades, the war meant dwindling of the population and economic ruin. In the end, Hangzhou, the capital of the Southern Song, fell in 1279, and the leader of the Mongols, Kublai Khan, proclaimed himself the emperor of China.

Yuan Dynasty (1271–1368)

The Yuan Dynasty was the first that represented an ethnic minority. After the initial phase of conquest and unrest, the beginning of the 14th century saw an era of peace. Trade and cultural exchange continued as the entirety of the Silk Road was now controlled by the Mongols. It was during that time when the Venetian traveler Marco Polo (ca. 1254–1324) traveled to China and described his exploits there. His journey and settlement in China were only a small fraction of the large influx of new settlers who now traveled through Asia undisturbed. Because the Mongols favored migrants over the local Chinese elite, the Yuan Dynasty was a period of flourishing of culture among the lower classes. This resulted in a new type of poetry and prose, written in a vernacular variety of the language.

Although the Chinese population was, understandably, not in favor of the Mongol dominance, the Yuan Dynasty saw no major political rebellions; instead, the rule of the Mongols was ended rather by natural disasters, such as the plague that killed an enormous part of the population. The rulers' inability to deal with the situation caused uprisings and forced the ruling class to flee China. A new dynasty, the Ming, was established.

Ming Dynasty (1368–1644)

The Ming Dynasty saw further development in the Chinese economy and cultural advancement. The population continued to grow, and the use of discoveries from the previous eras was perfected. The Great Wall of China was repaired and rebuilt, finally taking the iconic shape it has to this day.

After the period of being ruled by the Mongolian elite, the new emperors were slightly more hostile toward foreign influences in the court and among the population—but despite that, China's politics during that time wasn't isolationist. Chinese explorers and traders reached India, and cultural exchange with Japan was ever-going. As for the domestic policy, the Ming emperors promoted the development of agriculture and the creation of self-sufficient small communities. They also raised a massive army of over a million soldiers, a feat unattainable on that scale anywhere else in the world (Ebrey & Walthall, 2014). All these policies were aimed at strengthening the power of the imperial court as opposed to rich higher officials.

In terms of culture, classic Chinese novels flourished during the Ming Dynasty. Many of them introduced heroes who we will get to know in the latter chapters of this book—for instance, the 16th-century novel *Journey to the West* tells a story of a Buddhist monk traveling to India, incorporating many elements from the Chinese folk religion and mythology in the form of creatures and quests he meets on his way.

By the end of the Ming Dynasty, China's politics became increasingly isolationist. This was dictated by a variety of reasons, one of which was the increased activity of European, especially Portuguese, explorers and colonizers. At the end of the period, the Chinese fleet would often repel Portuguese, Dutch, and Japanese vessels from its shores.

The decline of the Ming Dynasty coincided with the emergence of a powerful state of Manchuria (northeast of China), whose rulers took over the imperial seat, establishing a new dynasty.

Qing Dynasty (1636–1912)

The long-standing Qing Dynasty was also the last imperial dynasty of China. It controlled enormous terrains spanning over Manchuria, China proper, and vast terrains to the west, forming the fourth largest empire in world history (Taagepera, 1997).

The height of the Qing Dynasty occurred in the 18th century, when the revenue from trade with European powers was bringing increasingly higher revenue and the Chinese technological advancements were compared and merged with the European ones. The literacy rate among the general population increased, and the publishing industry was growing. More women engaged in creative writing, especially poetry. A very important work for the study of Chinese mythology and folklore was written: a collection of short stories under the name *Strange Tales from a Chinese Studio*.

However, the tables turned in the 19th century, when a growing threat from the increasingly powerful British Empire led China to the Opium Wars, which forced the Chinese Empire to grant the British trade privileges and control of the ports; most crucially, opium was to be imported, threatening the stability of the country. Opium use and abuse became a societal problem. In Chinese historiography, these agreements are known as "unequal treaties" (Wang, 2008).

After a brief restoration period at the end of the 19th century, an anti-foreign rebellion of the so-called Boxers led, yet again, to an international intervention and an exhausting war. The new policies that the Qing government tried to instate afterwards failed as a growing class of intellectuals, aided by the military, started debating the end of the imperial rule and the institution of a republic. In 1912, after a successful uprising, the emperor was overthrown and China was proclaimed a republic.

The Republic of China and People's Republic of China (1912–modern day)

The first years of the Republic of China were marked by instability. In 1916, after the death of the military commander Yuan Shikai, a number of fragile coalitions were formed and the country was steering toward anarchy. The May Fourth Government was established in 1919 after World War I. Throughout the 1920s and 1930s, it promoted values such as nationalism, patriotism, and democracy. It was, however, anti-communist, and communist forces were already rather strong in China. For twenty years, from 1927 to 1949, China was ravaged by the Nationalist–Communist Civil War, which also lasted all throughout the Chinese involvement in World War II, known as the Second Sino-Japanese War (1937–1945). War crimes were committed by both sides of the conflict (Valentino, 2005).

In 1949, the Communists controlled most of China and established the People's Republic of China under the leadership of Mao Zedong. The old government fled to Taiwan, where it continued to be recognized as the legitimate government by the Western countries until the 1970s.

The communist economic plans, aimed at turning China into a "proper" communist society, caused a famine which ravaged the country, resulting in millions of deaths. In the 1960s, the Cultural Revolution reestablished a strong communist government; it lasted until Mao's death in 1976. Afterwards, the control of the government over the economy was slightly loosened, and the standard of living improved. That, however, didn't mean the end of the struggles: In 1989, the student protests at Tiananmen Square were dispelled and ended in a brutal massacre.

Throughout the majority of the 20th century, the belief in Chinese folklore stories stemming from the Chinese folk religion was frowned upon at best—a practice going back to the late Qing Dynasty, when the religion was viewed as "superstition"–and persecuted at worst. The Cultural Revolution aimed at a total eradication of religion–while in Taiwan, the old Republic of China government aimed at its preservation. After 1978, when many restrictions were lessened, Chinese folk religion experienced a comeback—and with it, all the practices and beliefs tied to the gods, spirits, and supernatural creatures.

After the Tiananmen Square massacre, a new generation of leaders took power in the People's Republic of China. This era was marked by higher cooperation with Western powers and by economic growth—making China what it is today. In modern day, even though the Chinese government remains highly controlling of its citizens, in terms of cultural heritage, many efforts are made to preserve and promote it—and that, of course, includes the preservation of traditional myths and folktales as well as their modern adaptations.

Chapter 2:

Creation

It is only right that we start our journey of Chinese mythology with the stories about the creation of the universe. Due to the multiplicity of religious and philosophical traditions, there is no single story that was preserved to our times—instead, in this chapter, I will give you several tales, from the oldest to the newest ones.

Tao Te Ching

Tao Te Ching is a philosophical text dating to around 405 B.C.E. and one of the fundamental texts for classic Taoism (Mair, 2012). Among other ideas and concepts related to Dao, it introduces the oldest known, rather poetic, description of creation. According to the text, Dao was at the beginning of all things, before time and the world were created. It was formless but also unchanging. Dao then gave birth to the concept of Unity, which, in turn, bore Duality—the origin of Yin and Yang, which, from then on, every creature would carry within itself. Duality, which can be also interpreted as a symbolic representation of Heaven and

Earth, then bore Trinity, and Trinity gave birth to innumerable creatures that populate the universe.

As we can see, this early text is philosophical rather than mythical in nature, and it doesn't mention any gods or supernatural beings. However, it's very important to the Chinese cosmogonic tradition, as the concepts of Unity and Duality will be present in later, more "colorful" creation stories.

Songs of Chu

The *Songs of Chu* is a collection of ancient Chinese poems, predominantly from the Han Dynasty. In a section of the book called the *Heavenly Questions*, a speaker addresses Heaven with a series of questions about mythology and the origins of the universe (Hawkes, 1968). The creation myth that emerges from these questions is somewhat similar to that from *Tao Te Ching*. In the beginning, there was a primeval element which constituted a formless expanse; then, a vapor emerged from it, slowly forming the upper and lower sphere, which would later become Heaven and Earth. These were the Yin and the Yang, and if they had stayed entirely separate, no further creation would have taken place. But Yin and Yang intermingled, and from that, the world was created. It is still being governed and ordered by the forces of that primeval duality. The *Heavenly Questions* describe the ordering of the universe in slightly more detail, though: The heavens are described as "ninefold" and standing on eight pillars, corresponding to eight directions, and the mountains would later be inhabited by various deities (Birrell, 1999).

Daoyuan

Daoyuan is yet another Daoist text; it dates to the 4th century B.C.E. (Birrell, 1999). Yet again, it describes Dao as a misty vapor from which all things were created. It places the emphasis on all creation being unified with Dao in the beginning, thus still bearing a part of Dao in themselves.

Huainanzi

Huainanzi is a collection of essays from the 2nd century B.C.E. (Liu & Major, 2010). The creation story included there focuses more on the nature of Yin and Yang.

According to the text, in the beginning, there was a formless flying and diving entity called the Grand Inception. Then, it gave way to Nebulous Void, which, in turn, produced the space-time continuum. The space-time produced *qi*, the vital force, or energy. It was the *qi* that later separated into Heaven and Earth since all light elements floated upwards, while all heavy mass fell downwards. Heaven and Earth was the beginning of Yin and Yang. The contrary nature of Yin and Yang, combined with their need to intermingle, created some strife and explosive atmospheric conditions: Various degrees of their mixtures produced the four seasons. Then, from these mixtures, creation sprung forward. Yin was the cold part of *qi*, and so it produced water and the Moon, and Yang was hot, so it gave us fire and the Sun.

It is possible that the abstract concepts of Yin and Yang were, in the beginning, representations of dualistic deities as it is the case in many cultures—but in time, and under the influence of Taoist philosophy, they were rationalized (Birrell, 1999).

Lingxian

Lingxian was written around 120. (Cullen, 2008). It contains a detailed description of the creation of the world, which aims at having a scientific feel to it. The description mostly follows what we already know from the *Huainanzi*—with the creation of *qi* from Dao and the separation of light and heavy elements—but presents it in a less mystical, or philosophical, and more physical, manner. Importantly, Heaven is described as being not simply above but around the Earth, which is round and heavy in this account. Heaven, the Yang, is also in a constant state of motion around the Earth. As we can see, this description is almost astronomical in matter, and although it gets the Earth's immobility wrong, it contains a few valid observations about our universe.

Nüwa and Fuxi

Finally, we are reaching a version of the creation myth that is less philosophical and more mythological— although, as we will see, this story doesn't take place before the world was created but shortly afterwards. It is parsed out from various sources, though the name of the goddess Nüwa also appears in the *Songs of Chu* (Hawkes, 1968), and the *Huainanzi* contains, apart from the astronomic creation story, also her story (Liu & Major, 2010).

But let us start with Fuxi. Along with Nüwa, his twin sister, he was a son of Huaxu, a powerful being, and after the separation of Heaven from the Earth, lived in the sky. Both Fuxi and Nüwa had the upper body of people and the lower body of snakes.

Nüwa was to become a mother goddess—but not quite yet. After Heaven and Earth were separated and the eight pillars of the sky were created, it turned out that they were made of an unstable material. They cracked and fell, damaging the Earth very badly. Fires and floods occurred. There are some versions of the myth that say it was a battle between the Immortals that caused the pillars to crumble. But however it had happened, they were now in tatters, and the Earth was under a serious threat.

So, Nüwa decided to create a new building material. She gathered stones in five different colors, according to the principle of *wuxing*: a concept in Chinese philosophy that describes five elements or cosmic agents creating the universe. Those elements are: fire, water, earth, wood, and metal.

Then, Nüwa patched up the sky with the stones. For the pillars, she used the legs of Ao, a giant turtle who lived in the sea as well as the body of a black dragon. Then, she embraced Fuxi who was still living in the sky; he was her brother and consort. Their embrace further solidified the balance in the universe.

Then, Nüwa became the mother goddess. She formed humanity from yellow clay, creating each person individually, lovingly forming them by her own hands. And so, her love for the world and for the people living in it preserved the universe as we know it today.

Pangu

I have saved the most popular creation myth to the end of this chapter. It was first recorded in the 3rd century (Birrell, 1999).

The story of Pangu joins with that of Nüwa and Fuxi. It precedes the Nüwa story chronologically when it comes to the order of the universe but was written down centuries after it.

The story of Pangu gives a more folkloristic aspect to the Taoist story of the chaotic vapors and the separation of Heaven from Earth. According to the tale, the chaos that existed in the universe before the creation of Heaven and Earth was confined within the shape of an enormous egg. Inside, a giant named Pangu was sleeping soundly, and for many an age. But one day, he awoke and separated Heaven from the Earth. He achieved this through a series of nine transformations: Each day, he grew a little taller, lifting the Heaven on his arms just a little bit higher.

But the "days" in the early universe reckoning weren't literal days; instead, they constituted very long ages. In fact, it took Pangu 18,000 years to rise to his full height. But Pangu, even though extremely long-lived, was not immortal; soon after he rose, his old age approached, leading him to death. And now, his body decomposed, various parts of it forming various elements of the world: His left eye became the Sun, and his right eye, the Moon; his breath turned into wind and clouds; his voice became thunder; his legs and hands spread out into four cardinal directions, becoming four mountains at the edge of the world; his blood and semen turned into rivers, his muscles into the earth and dirt, while his skin became the land. His body hair turned into vegetation, and his bones and teeth into rocks and metal. His sweat poured down on the Earth in the form of the first rainfall. And lastly, the fleas on Pangu's body turned into people.

Chapter 3:

All From the One—Gods

and Goddesses

God of Heaven, the Great Oneness

Traditional Chinese theology claims that all beings arose from one god. The God of Heaven can sometimes be equated with the concept of Heaven itself—the ancient character for Heaven, Tiān, is one of his names (Chang, 2000). Another name, Shangdi, means "Supreme Deity," and it's believed that it was developed during the Shang Dynasty (Eno, 2008). Another name for the God of Heaven is Yudi, or Jade Emperor, and this version of his figure is the most vividly described (Lagerwey & Kalinowski, 2009). The God of Heaven has many more names, all reflecting his omnipresence, superiority, and oneness.

Ti□n and Shangdi

As Tiān or Shangdi, the God of Heaven is not one of the pagan gods we are used to from many mythological traditions. He isn't made in a human's image; instead, he much more resembles the one God of monotheistic religions. He is transcendent, meaning that he is separate from the universe he created, and prefers to work through lesser gods instead. He is the source of all goodness, and he controls everything that happens under the sky. But he also gives challenges and other tasks to humans so that, by performing them, they might become more virtuous.

During the Shang Dynasty, the cult of the God of Heaven was vitally important. Prayers, rituals, and sacrifices to him would be made before battles—especially by the current ruler of China—as well as during the harvest season. He was also believed to control the flooding of the Yellow River—a natural phenomenon vital to the agriculture of the region. He ruled the land of the living as well as the dead—he was the king of the underworld.

Archaeological evidence has shown that in the beginnings of ancient China, after a sacrifice was made to the God of Heaven—most commonly, oxen would be sacrificed—a shoulder blade of the sacrificed animal would be extracted and thrown into fire (Xu, 2002). Then, a question to the god would be asked, and the pattern of smoke and fire around the bone would be interpreted as the deity's answer.

Over time, the mentions of the God of Heaven became more and more abstract and impersonal—until he was conflated with Heaven itself. When Christian missionaries came to China during the Ming Dynasty, they started using the concept of the God of Heaven to explain the idea of the Christian God. There were, of course, many differences between the traditional Chinese and the Christian concept—but the name Shangdi or Tiān became, nonetheless, associated with the Abrahamic God—or with a concept of a singular omnipotent god in general (Lee, 2005).

Jade Emperor

The version of the God of Heaven as the Jade Emperor is, as I have already mentioned, the most vivid one and the most resembling of a god from a polytheistic mythology. Instead of being an omnipresent god with no origin, he was a king of Heaven who, nonetheless, had a birth. It is said that from early childhood, he was pure of heart and benevolent and always helped those in need. At that time, the Earth was a dangerous place: Various monsters and demons roamed its confines, and Yudi tried to help the people escape their clutches as much as he could. But he couldn't erase their suffering entirely, so, after some time, he retreated into the mountains, where he cultivated the ways of Dao.

But while Yudi was contemplating, an evil monster took over the rule of the Earth. Having himself contemplated Dao in order to gain power—though admittedly, for a shorter time than Yudi—he then amassed an army of demons and took control of the poor people. At last, he even planned to conquer Heaven.

The immortal beings living in Heaven were terrified. They tried to stop the evil monster as much as they could, but they lost the war. Heaven was conquered.

And that was precisely when Yudi emerged from his meditation. He now knew all the ways of the Dao and, therefore, was aware how to change the living conditions on the Earth in order to make life for the people more bearable. So he sat down to work.

But while he was reshaping the Earth, he looked up, into the sky, and noticed an odd glow coming from it. Instantly, he knew that something was wrong. Swiftly, he jumped up to Heaven, and seeing what was happening, he challenged the evil monster to a single combat. Now that he was equipped with all the ways of Dao, he had no difficulty winning over the evil immortal who had trained in the Way for a shorter time than him. After his victory, Yudi was proclaimed the king of Heaven.

When he ascended the throne of Heaven, Yudi adopted and cultivated the principles of Dao. Being extremely long-lived, he reigned a hundred million years, after which he gained immortality and became known as the Jade Emperor.

There are several other stories involving the Jade Emperor. In one of them, *The Cowherd and the Weaver Girl*, he had seven daughters, one of them being Zhinü, the goddess of the star Vega (Brown & Brown, 2006). Every day, she would weave the silver threads forming the Milky Way, and after her work was done, she would descend into the Earth in order to bathe.

One day, Niu Liang, a simple peasant and a cowherd, was passing a river when he saw the beautiful Zhinü bathing. Instantly, he fell in love with her. But he was also clever and somewhat sneaky: He saw Zhinü's celestial robe laying on the river bank, and he guessed that without it, the goddess would be unable to return to Heaven. So he stole it. When Zhinü emerged from the water and realized the robe wasn't there, she panicked; but immediately, Niu Liang grabbed her and carried her to his home.

It is said that although Zhinü was initially unwilling, she finally fell in love with Niu Liang and married him. And that is when the Jade Emperor, who had been looking for his daughter, found out about the whole affair: Since the couple had already married, he could do nothing and was greatly angered.

But Zhinü, even though her life wasn't miserable, still missed her father. One day, as she was cleaning the house, she found her celestial robe, stashed in a box. She decided to pay her father a visit.

But when Zhinü reached Heaven, the Jade Emperor caught her and then caused a river to flow across the Milky Way so that the goddess couldn't return to the Earth. Zhinü despaired and begged her father for mercy; at last, the Emperor relented a bit. He allowed the lovers to meet only once a year, on the seventh day of the seventh month of the lunar calendar. This explains why the Milky Way seems to be dimmer on that particular day of the year: The river temporarily doesn't separate the two lovers. On that day in China, people celebrate the Qixi festival; similar to the Western Valentine's Day, it is the feast of lovers (Brown & Brown, 2006).

Another story involving the Jade Emperor is an origin story of the 12 animals associated with the Chinese zodiac. It is said that after eons of ruling Heaven, the Emperor forgot how the Earth looked, and so one day, out of curiosity, he ordered the most prominent animals of the Earth to come up and visit him in Heaven. So, all the important animals gathered and walked up in a procession: the Ox, the Tiger, the Rabbit, the Dragon, the Snake, the Horse, the Goat, the Monkey, the Rooster, and the Dog. But there were two more animals: the Cat and the Rat. On the day of the procession, the Cat, who had a tendency to oversleep, asked his friend the Rat to wake him up and walk with him in a pair. The Rat, however, was worried. The Cat was such a beautiful animal, and he was scared that he would pale in comparison and that the Emperor would laugh at him. So he didn't wake the Cat up, and at the last minute, the animal had to be replaced with the Pig. This story explains why, to this day, cats and rats are great enemies of each other.

Yin and Yang Gods

Since in traditional Taoist cosmology, duality arose from oneness, it is not surprising that we can find pairs of opposing and intermingling gods in Chinese mythology. We have already mentioned Nüwa and Fuxi—but there is more than one pair of such deities.

Nüwa and Fuxi

Coming back to the half-human, half-snake creators of humanity, let us talk about other properties of that primordial divine pair.

It is said that after Nüwa created humans from the yellow clay, Fuxi invented all the activities that the people were about to occupy themselves with: hunting and fishing, domestication of animals, cooking, and performing music. Interestingly, in one of the Confucian texts from the 1st century, the society before Fuxi introduced it to those concepts was described as matriarchal, as Nüwa presided over everything (Adcock, 2003). The text interprets this state of things as chaotic and unruly because men didn't know how to hunt or fish properly and they didn't perform sacrifices to the gods, nor did they know the institution of marriage. But it is interesting to see the idea of a matriarchal society preceding the patriarchal one—perhaps an echo of some actual pre-historical society whose records are lost to time?

Wen and Wu Gods

Wen and Wu are, again, gods who resemble concepts more than persons. They symbolize the opposition—and the complementary nature of—the civil and the military sphere. The concepts of Wen and Wu have been used in Chinese law and in the areas of government. Over time, various gods have been associated with the concepts of Wen and Wu, but the two most famous ones are Wenchang Wang, the god of culture and literature, and Chiyou, the god of war.

Several accounts about Wenchang Wang cite him as a human hero who was deified after death (Christie, 1968). He was supposed to have lived several times, and in different historical periods; sometimes, he would live as a spirit and people would visit him, searching for his prophecies about the future.

Wenchang Wang is noble of heart and incorruptible. He is also wise and was so even as a human; he was born already at a full mental capacity. Known for his compassion, he helps all those who found themselves in a tight spot.

Because of his wisdom, Wenchang Wang is worshiped as a patron of students and scholars. But historically, not only the higher educated class would venerate him—he would be called upon by the rich and the poor alike.

Contrary to Wenchang Wang, Chiyou was a supernatural hero before becoming a god, a son of naked flame. He lived in the times of the legendary emperors and took part in several battles against them. He defeated the god Shennong, who had to resort to the help of the mythical Yellow Emperor. It was the Yellow Emperor who finally defeated Chiyou—after 10 years of battle, during which Chiyou breathed out fumes which obscured the sun. It was only when the Yellow Emperor invented a new battle device—a chariot that always pointed south—that he was able to defeat Chiyou. The hero was killed, but that was only the beginning of his worship as the god of war.

It is no wonder that Chiyou was so difficult to beat: He has four eyes and six arms, and his head is made of bronze. During his life, he would boast that he was impossible to conquer and managed to escape unscathed even when the goddess Nüwa dropped a boulder on his head.

Xiwangmu and Dongwanggong

Xiwangmu and Dongwanggong, also known as Queen Mother of the West and King Father of the East, are an alternative pair of parent, opposing, and complimentary deities. In Taoism, the king represents the Yang, and the queen the Yin. In an alternative version of the myth about humanity, the love between Xiwangmu and Dongwanggong created the first people (Roberts, 2010).

Xiwangmu was the goddess of the mountains. She held her court on Mount Kunlun in western China; in the middle of her palace, there was a huge stone pillar which allowed for communications between Heaven and Earth. She also had an orchard full of supernatural peach trees, and if she allowed her guests to take a fruit from them, they would attain immortality.

Dongwanggong, on the other hand, lived in a huge stone house in the easternmost mountain of China. He had white hair and was 10 feet high, and his face was the face of a bird. He would ride around his domain on a huge black bear.

The two deities could only meet each other thanks to the stone pillar at Xiwangmu's palace. When Xiwangmu first climbed the pillar, she found Dongwanggong hiding under the right wing of a huge bird that was sitting on top of it. This was the only place where the East and the West could meet, producing humanity from their union.

Other Gods and Goddesses

Bixia Yuanjun

Bixia is the goddess of childbirth, dawn, and destiny. Her place of residence is Mount Tai in Shandong Province, which is a part of the mountain range known as Sacred Mountains of China—a place of special historic and religious significance.

Bixia is a powerful goddess. She not only guards a person's life when they are born but right up to the point of their death—and she also rules over the realm of the dead. Over time, she only gained importance, especially during the Ming and Qing Dynasties, when she was worshiped profusely at the imperial court and became very important for northern China. During that time, she merged with various lesser-standing mother goddesses, including Guanyin, a Buddhist Bodhisattva (a lesser goddess or a person on their way to spiritual awakening).

In many versions of the legends tied to Bixia, she is the daughter of the God of Heaven, although there are also some versions that try to historicize her, attributing her parentage to various historical figures.

Doumu

Doumu is the goddess of Heaven and could even be interpreted as a female aspect of the God of Heaven—or as his mother or wife. She presides over the constellation of the Great Dipper, and the seven stars that form it are said to be her seven sons. Some myths also credit her with birthing the Yellow Emperor—one of the legendary Chinese emperors whose stories we will learn in Chapter 5.

After the introduction of Buddhism into China, Doumu was conflated with another Buddhist Bodhisattva, Marici, who was also the queen of the Great Dipper.

Pangu

We have already met Pangu, the creator giant, in Chapter 2, when he awoke from the cosmic egg, separated Heaven from the Earth, and when his body became the Earth's landscape after his death. Here, let us add another bit to the story, originating from southern China, from among the Bouyei people. They hold a belief that before his death, Pangu fell in love and married the daughter of a powerful god known as the Dragon King (more about him in a bit). The Bouyei believe that they originated from that union.

But Pangu's firstborn son was unruly and disrespected his mother. Wounded by this, she ran away to Heaven, to her father the Dragon King. Pangu was so heartbroken by this that he grew weak; he remarried, but he didn't love his second wife. In the end, he died on the sixth day of the sixth month of the Chinese lunar calendar, a day that would later become an important ancestral holiday for the Bouyei.

Shennong

Shennong is a very important deity in Chinese mythology. He is the god of agriculture but also medicine. Along with Nüwa and Fuxi, he is counted among the so-called Three Sovereigns: the first three mythical rulers of the Earth before the time of the five legendary emperors and before the official chronicling of China's history. According to this classification, Fuxi was the Heavenly Sovereign, Nüwa—the Earthly Sovereign, and Shennong—the Sovereign of Humanity, also known as the Flame Emperor (Hucker, 2008).

Shennong was a culture hero: a mythical being accredited with teaching humanity a skill necessary for the development of a civilization. In this particular case, Shennong is said to have taught people a whole array of skills connected to agriculture and husbandry: He invented a hoe, an ax, and a plow as well as taught humans how to dig wells and irrigate their fields. Because of his close ties to the cultivation of plants, Shennong also unveiled medicinal properties of many herbs—and that is why he started to be venerated as the god of medicine as well. It is said that he had to teach himself before he taught humans and that he swallowed several poisonous plants, sacrificing his health for the good of his subjects (Wu, 1982).

Shennong is believed to be the father of the Yellow Emperor—the legendary father of all Chinese imperial dynasties. As we already mentioned, he was defeated in an epic battle by the god of war Chiyou. But according to another version of the story, he died when he swallowed one poisonous plant too many and was unable to get the antidote in time. But this only solidified his position as the god of healing and agriculture, the protector of humanity. Because of Shennong's experiments, the authorship of the first Chinese book on medicines, *Shennong Ben Cao Jing*—a compilation written down between ca. 206 B.C.E. and 220 C.E.—is attributed to him (Unschuld, 1986).

Yanwang

Yanwang, or King Yan, is the god of the dead. He is the ruler of Diyu, the Chinese underworld.

The concept of Diyu cannot be likened to the Christian hell; if anything, it resembles more the purgatory. It's said to be constructed as a maze-like prison with numerous chambers into which the souls are led in order to purge themselves from their imperfections, ascending from one chamber to another, before they are reincarnated. The concept of Diyu was influenced predominantly by Taoist and Buddhist traditions.

King Yan resides in the capital of Diyu, called Youdu. It is an underground place which is organized similarly to an earthly city. It has walls and courts, including the court of justice where King Yan pronounces punishments for the souls.

King Yan features most prominently in one of the classic Chinese novels *Journey to the West* (Wu & Yu, 2012). Among many tales, it tells a story of Sun Wukong, also known as the Monkey King (more about him in the next chapter). One day, he had a dream about two guardians of Diyu carrying his soul there. Angered that the deities decided his time had come, Sun Wukong beat the guardians and then rode himself to the very gates of Diyu. He forced his way before King Yan and complained about his attendants who had tried to unjustly imprison him in the realm of the dead. King Yan, taken by his outspokenness, said that a mistake had been made—after all, the world is vast, and there are many people bearing the same name. Gladdened by this, Sun Wukong wiped away his name from the Book of Life and Death—a tome that governs the life of every mortal—becoming the only person capable of evading death.

Yinyanggong

Yinyanggong, as can be guessed from his name, symbolizes the unity between Yin and Yang. As such, he makes sure order is upheld both on Earth and in the underworld. As a deity who is able to see both sides of the universe, he is often depicted with a face divided into a white and a black part. But he mostly takes care of the underworld when the rightful lord of the place is occupied.

Gods of Natural Phenomena

There is a separate category of gods in Chinese mythology who are titular deities of various meteorological and other natural phenomena. There are as many of them as the incidents that could occur in nature—here, we will tell stories about the most prominent and interesting ones.

Dragon King

Dragon King, whom I have already mentioned in relation to Pangu, is perhaps one of the most important natural deities in Chinese myth. He is the god of water but also of weather in general. He is the one responsible for rainfall.

Despite his title, the Dragon King can be depicted as a human as well as a dragon. He is mostly venerated during the fifth and sixth month of the Chinese calendar, when multiple processions and boat races are said to ensure the appropriate weather for the rest of the year.

We will talk more about the concept of the Chinese dragon in the next chapter. The Dragon King, even though he can be venerated as a singular figure, also has variants in the form of multiple Dragon Kings responsible for various regions of the world, such as the Five Dragon Kings of five Chinese regions and the Four Dragon Kings of four seas. We will talk about them all in a bit.

Hòutǔ

Hòutǔ is the goddess of the Earth. In Taoism, she complements the Jade Emperor; with him and two other gods of the North Star and the Little Dipper, she forms a group of Four Heavenly Ministers.

But Hòutǔ can also be presented as male. As such, he is the son of a water deity, and he controls the floods; his natural element is the earth.

Leishen

Leishen, or Leigong, is the god of thunder. He acts as a judge and a punisher: He strikes down humans and spirits who had gained the secret knowledge of the ways of Dao and used it to harm others.

Leishen rides a heavenly chariot, assisted by his wife Dianmu and a couple of servants. His appearance is fearsome, complete with bat wings and sharp claws. As he rides, Dianmu holds up a mirror, which reflects the light, forming lightning. At the same time, his three servants are also working hard: One of them whips the clouds to create a gloomy storm atmosphere; another slashes through buckets of rain with his sword, causing rainfall; and the third one blows into a goatskin bag, producing a mighty wind.

There is one interesting story tied to Leishen and to the origin of his divinity. He wasn't always a god; he was born a human. But one day, as he was out on a stroll, he chanced upon a peach tree. It had grown from a divine seed that fell from Heaven when some fox spirits were having a fight. Leishen ate one of the peaches from the tree, and immediately he was transformed into a bat-like creature.

Then, he was brought before the Jade Emperor. The God of Heaven commanded Leishen to use his newfound power wisely: He was only to strike bad people with his lightning.

The problem was, whenever Leishen rode out into the storm, the sky was darkened considerably by the clouds, and the newly appointed god couldn't see properly. So sometimes, he would strike good people by accident, and that is what one day happened to Dianmu, a daughter of a rice farmer.

Dianmu left her house. She was carrying a bag of rice, and she stopped by a river to wet it, as it was too hard for her mother to eat. From the sky, Leishen saw the girl dumping the rice into water. Lacking context, he thought that Dianmu was wasting food. Enraged, he immediately struck her with his lightning. The girl died on the spot.

When the Jade Emperor heard about this, he was angry. It had not been the first time that Leishen had made a mistake. As a conciliatory gesture, the Jade Emperor revived the poor girl and made her into a goddess. From then on, she became Leishen's consort: Leishen's punishment was to care for the person he had recklessly killed. Now, Dianmu rides the chariot with Leishen, and by the use of her lightning mirrors—which always come before the actual strike of lightning—she ensures that only the wrongdoers get killed.

Mazu

Mazu is a sea goddess. Before she became deified, though, she used to be a mortal—a shamaness from a small fishing village in Fujian in southeastern China who lived in the 10th century (Clark, 2007). Not much else is known about her life from a historical point of view—but there are many legends connected to her mortal life.

It is said that Mazu showed signs of wisdom and insight from an early age. She didn't cry when she was born, nor in the first days after her birth, and until the age of four, she was a very quiet child. She was born to an ordinary family of Buddhist fishermen, albeit one that was well-liked among their neighbors. According to some versions of the legends, Mazu wasn't even born in a conventional way but, instead, emerged from her mother's womb in the form of a beam of light.

Mazu soon became well-versed in all types of religious traditions. When she was eight, she knew Confucius' teachings by heart, and by eleven, she mastered the

Buddhist sutras, or prayers (Yuan, 2006). One of her masters was a Buddhist monk named Xuantong, who realized that she had the makings of a Buddha and gifted her a book of lore that allowed her to see the future and travel into far-away places in spirit.

Mazu soon started using her abilities to achieve the ends that would later make her the goddess of the sea. She was an exceptional swimmer, and with her newfound powers, she was now able to guard the fishermen's ships safely to the shore, even in adverse weather conditions. Soon, she also gained other powers, such as the ability to bring rain in the times of drought.

One day, when Mazu was 16, the members of her family, including her brothers and her father, went out fishing. As they were away at sea, the weather started rapidly deteriorating. Mazu's mother was very worried about them, but Mazu, who had been weaving cloth at her loom, fell into a trance. Her spirit traveled far into the sea and started saving the men from the waves. But Mazu's mother, who was unaware of what her daughter was doing, shook her arm, not understanding why Mazu was unresponsive to her expressed worries. This caused Mazu to drop one of her brothers back into the sea. The rest of the men were saved and came back home to relate the whole incident.

Mazu is believed to have died when she was either 27 or 28 (Clark, 2007). She was unmarried, and she passed away during a meditation, after which she immediately ascended into Heaven as a goddess. She soon started to be worshiped as a protective sea deity. The first attestations of her cult come from the 12th century (Clark, 2007).

There is also a legend tied to Mazu as a goddess. When she ascended, she immediately met other numerous sea deities, among them two sea demons, who immediately fell in love with her. But Mazu was determined to stay a virgin even after her mortal life, so she said she would marry only someone who defeated her in combat. She then bested both of the demons, subdued them, and employed them as her generals.

Mazu's cult is still very prominent in China today— even to the point of Mazuism becoming a separate religious tradition—and her temples attract many pilgrims. Her festival is held on the ninth day of the ninth month of the Chinese lunar calendar—which is believed to be the day when she ascended to Heaven.

Sanxing

The Sanxing is the common name for three star deities, responsible for the stars of Jupiter, Ursa Major, and Canopus, respectively. Their names are Fu, Lu, and Shou. They are always represented in art as three old, bearded men and are believed to bring good fortune to those who pray to them, especially during the Chinese New Year. Individually, each of the gods represents a different concept.

Fu, or Fuxing, is the personification of Fortune. As the planet Jupiter, he is considered auspicious. He can also be a patron of scholars and children, being often depicted surrounded by them with a scroll in his hand. It is believed that during his mortal life, he was an official during the Tang Dynasty who risked his life to protect his subjects. He is believed to bring wealth to those who pray to him.

Lu, or Luxing, is the symbol of Prosperity. It is said that as a mortal, he lived during the Shu Dynasty and was an important government official—therefore, he is the god of influence, power, and rank.

Finally, Shou, or Shouxing, stands for Longevity. In Chinese astronomy, the star Canopus represents the South Pole, and it is rather significant. It is believed to control the lifespans of humans. For this reason, Shou is often depicted as the oldest of the three gods, with his beard long and white and with a peach-like forehead (representing the peaches of immortality owned by the goddess Xiwangmu), and he is known as the Old Man of the South Pole. It is believed that as a mortal, he was either sitting in his mother's womb for 10 years and emerged from it already as an old man (Zhelyazkov, 2022) or was a sickly boy who gave offering to the gods and managed to bargain with them to live 91 instead of 19 years as had been planned (Allen, 2019).

Wen Shen

Wen Shen can either be presented as a single god or as a group of deities. He is the god of plague who is said to command five spirits, known as the Five Commissioners of Pestilence. Four of them appear in four corners of China during the four seasons of the year, while the fifth one is responsible for the center of the country, and all year round.

According to one legend, at least three of the five spirits had been born as people, being the sons of Zhuanxu, one of the legendary emperors of China. But they died soon after their births and became the spirits of plague.

The god and the spirits of the plagues are never senseless. They are said to unleash pestilence only as a punishment for people's bad behavior, and they can be placated with rituals and prayers, not only individually, but also performed by whole communities, such as villages.

Xihe

Xihe is the goddess of the sun and the mother of mythical creatures, three-legged crows, that symbolize the sun. With them, she travels every day in a golden chariot driven by dragons. After dusk, she rests in the mythical East Sea, where her crows perch on a supernatural mulberry tree called the Fusang.

Gods of Crafts and Human Virtues

Baosheng Dadi

Baosheng Dadi is the god of medicine, and he is a deified human. As a man, his name was Wu Tao, and he was believed to have been born in 979 in a small village in Fujian Province (Predagio, 2008). He was a skilled physician who applied the principles of Dao to his craft. He not only healed people but also animals and other creatures. He is said to have removed a foreign object from the throat of a tiger as well as healed a blind dragon by applying special eye drops. Not long after his death, Wu Tao began to be worshiped as a god. This worship was made official in the 15th century.

B☐xi☐n

The term Bāxiān refers to a group of deities rather than a single god. They are the Eight Immortals who can give life and destroy evil. All of them are said to have been humans once, most of them born either during Tang or Song Dynasty. They achieved their status as Immortals thanks to practicing the ways of Dao. Today, they live on the very peak of Mount Penglai in eastern China, in a sort of paradise on Earth.

The names and stories of the Eight Immortals are as follows.

He Xiangu

He Xiangu is the only woman among the Immortals. She lived during the Tang Dynasty and was an ordinary woman, if not for the fact that she was born with six long hairs on her scalp. One day, when He Xiangu was 15, she had a dream: A divine figure appeared to her and told her that if she ate powdered mica stone, she would become immortal. She agreed to do so, additionally engaging in the practice of Bigu—a Taoist fasting practice through gradually decreasing one's food intake—and vowing to forever remain a virgin. Soon, her fame reached far and wide, and she was even summoned to the imperial court by Wu Zetian (624–705), one of the only ruling empresses in Chinese history. But He Xiangu disappeared on the way and ascended to Heaven, where she was transformed into an immortal goddess.

Cao Guojiu

The next Immortal on our list is Cao Guojiu. He was the younger brother of Empress Cao (1016–1079) of Song Dynasty. As such, he, as well as their other brother Cao Jingzhi enjoyed a special status in society.

But unlike Cao Guojiu who knew that as a member of the imperial family, he held responsibilities as well as privileges, Cao Jingzhi abused his power. He would promote corruption and use his status to bully people. Cao Guojiu tried to persuade him to change but without result. So the only other thing left for Cao Guojiu was to use his influence and fortune to help the poor and repair at least some of the damage done by his brother. But one day Cao Jingzhi had done one too many misdeeds and was accused before the imperial court. Ashamed for his brother, Cao Guojiu retreated from the palace and became a recluse in the countryside. There, he engaged in the ways of Dao and eventually became an Immortal.

Li Tieguai

The third of the Immortals is Li Tieguai. He is one of the most popular among the group. He is said to have studied Dao under Laozi, a semilegendary Taoist philosopher, in the 3rd century B.C.E. Laozi put Li Tieguai through a number of tests: First, he conjured a beautiful young woman to tempt him;, but Li Tienguai refused to acknowledge her presence. For this, Laozi gave him a little pill, the consummation of which meant Li Tieguai would never again suffer hunger or illness.

Next, Laozi tempted Li Tieguai with money: He created a ruse in which he prompted some robbers to bury sacks of money near Li Tieguai's abode, while he knew that Li Tieguai would be watching. Then, he disguised himself as a beggar-prophet and told Li Tieguai that he should take any money that would come to him.

But again, Li Tieguai refused. He said that he didn't care if he was poor his entire life, virtue was more important. Laozi then revealed himself and congratulated his pupil, giving him another pill. This time, after Li Tieguai swallowed it, his spirit could fly in the air at a very rapid speed. So, he flew up to Heaven itself, having told his attendant Li Qing that if he didn't return after seven days, the man was to bury his body, as it meant that he had become immortal.

But Li Qing only waited for six days and a half. After that time, he suddenly got news that his mother was gravely ill and if he didn't hurry to go and see her immediately, she might die never seeing her son again. So Li Qing swiftly cremated Li Tieguai's body—after all, it had *almost* been seven days—and hurried to see his mother.

At that point, Li Tieguai came back from Heaven. His spirit had no body to come back to. But as it happened, a poor, ugly beggar had just died of starvation nearby;

his body was the only available one for Li Tieguai to inhabit. So Li Tieguai, foregoing his pride—his own body had been rather handsome—possessed the body of the beggar.

In that guise, he met Laozi. His master recognized him immediately and gave him a third pill. This time, it was a never-emptying medicine gourd that could cure any illness. Li Tieguai, having heard what had befallen Li Qing's mother, went to her home and cured her. He then dismissed Li Qing from his service; the man hadn't been a good servant, but at the same time, his care for his mother was more than understandable. So Li Tieguai promised him that if he worked hard at practicing the ways of Dao, he would one day become an immortal himself—something that later indeed proved true.

Now, finally, Li Tieguai was ready to become one of the Immortals. He would from now on be known for his all-curing medicine, traveling the confines of the world to cure the sick. Today, he is still revered in many traditional Chinese pharmacies and apothecaries: An iron crutch, Li Tieguai's symbol and one of the items Laozi had given him before parting ways, often hangs before the entrance of such traditional places.

Lan Caihe

Lan Caihe is an interesting case—the only one of the Eight Immortals who doesn't have a specified gender. Some accounts present them as an intersex person, others as a person whom we would now consider to be genderfluid—and yet others as a man who looked like a woman.

They are said to have lived during the Tang Dynasty but are not based on any particular historical or legendary figure. During their mortal life, they were supposed to have been a street entertainer and homeless. They sang philosophical songs and produced music using traditional clapping instruments, similar to castanets, as well as cymbals. They would also carry around a basket full of flowers, distributing them among the people—which made them a patron of florists. All these activities are something that Lan Caihe would continue after being elevated to the rank of an Immortal.

But how did Lan Caihe become an Immortal? During their life, their songs, though entertaining, were regarded by the listeners as nonsensical—even more so because Lan acted as if they were drunk or even mad, both their gender presence and their behavior falling out of the rules of society. However, the song's content was actually rather sophisticated, talking about the Taoist principles of rejecting pleasurable life and accepting the way of an ascetic. Chiefly out of pity, many spectators paid Lan Caihe when they performed, but they only used the money to pay for their food and drink, never allowing themselves any earthly pleasures. The rest of the money, they gave to the poor.

Soon, people started noticing unusual things about Lan. They never seemed to be cold, even when wearing very light clothing during winter. Similarly, they roamed the roads of China and performed for years, and then decades, but they never seemed to age, always resembling a youth of around 16 or 17. And yet, Lan Caihe was not Immortal.

But one day, they were drinking in a tavern when they suddenly heard a beautiful pipe song. In a flash, a crane landed on Lan's table. Lan grabbed its wings, and they both flew up to Heaven. As they took off, Lan lost their sandal, but when an onlooker tried to take it, it disappeared.

There are several stories tied to Lan Caihe from after they became an Immortal, as well. It is said that when it happened, they received a special clapping instrument made out of jade and used it to ride across the Eastern Sea to the abode of the Eight Immortals. But they were spotted by one of the Dragon Kings who lived in the Eastern Sea. The dragon envied Lan Caihe their instrument, so he jumped out of the sea, caught Lan Caihe, and imprisoned them.

This was the beginning of a war between the dragons and the Immortals, a long and dramatic conflict. In the end, the Immortals had to push their mountain into the sea, in order to ruin their underwater palace. Lan Caihe was rescued.

Lü Dongbin

Lü Dongbin is the leader of the Eight Immortals. As a mortal, he was a scholar during the Tang Dynasty and was born around 796 (Stepanchuk & Choy, 1991). It is said that soon after his birth, a very pleasant fragrance filled the room where he was laying as a sign of his extraordinary future. From early childhood, he was very intelligent and quick to learn—but even despite that, he failed the imperial exam for a civil servant.

He became a lower official. But soon, this life turned out odious to him, and he retreated into the mountainous countryside to contemplate the ways of Dao. But he was still unhappy at the fact that he hadn't passed the exams and didn't become a high-ranking official.

One day, he walked down to the city and into an inn, where he ordered a millet to be cooked for him. As he was waiting for his meal, he dozed off and had the strangest dream. In the dream, he passed the examination with honors and everyone was so impressed with him that he soon became a vice minister. To add to his success, he chose a bride from a very rich household and was soon married. Years passed in the dream, and Lü Dongbin was getting promoted again and again until at last he became the prime minister.

But he was not happy. Other people were jealous of his success, and he had no true friends. His rivals conspired against him until at last he was falsely accused of a crime and thrown out of his office. Even his wife betrayed him. In the dream, Lü Dongbin also had children, but they were soon attacked by bandits and died. At last, he lost all his money and became a beggar on the street. Just as he was about to die of starvation, Lü Dongbin woke up.

Dazed, he came back to reality. Even though years had passed in the dream, here, his millet was still not quite ready yet. Lü Dongbin blinked and pondered on his vision: He realized that the dreams about success and riches were always treacherous and that one shouldn't place too much of an importance on earthly glory. Now fully satisfied, Lü Dongbin came back to his mountainous abode to study the ways of Dao more diligently.

Lü Dongbin's master was Zhongli Quan, another one of the Eight Immortals, of whom we'll talk in a bit. He created a number of tests for Lü Dongbin, 10 in total; they all were aimed at perfecting his skill in Dao.

The first trial was supposed to test Lü Dongbin's stoicism in the face of misfortune. One day, as he came back to his abode, he found a loved member of his family on their deathbed. But instead of lamenting, he peacefully accepted this fate and started preparing for the burial. Zhongli Quan then revived the member of Lü's family and told him that he had passed the test.

The second trial tested Lü Dongbin's meekness. He had made a bargain with a merchant, but when it came to handling his product, the merchant refused to pay in full. Instead of arguing, Lü Dongbin accepted this. He passed the test.

During the third test, Lü Dongbin gave some money to a beggar. But instead of being grateful, the beggar demanded more and, after some time, even started shouting obscenities at Lü. But Lü just left, smiling; this test taught him that he should give alms even if those whom he helped didn't display gratitude.

For the fourth test, Lü became a shepherd. One day, a tiger attacked his flock, but instead of flying from the scene, Lü defended his sheep with his own body. Awed by his bravery, the tiger, who had been sent by Zhongli Quan, left without harming Lü.

The fifth test tried Lü Dongbin's virtue. As he was studying, a beautiful woman came by and tried to flirt with him—but he remained untempted.

During the sixth test, Lü came back from his daily work to his home and found it completely destroyed and ravaged by bandits. Instead of despairing, he set out to work on rebuilding his house. As he was digging in the ground, he found many pieces of gold, which allowed him to rebuild without any damage being done to his finances.

The seventh trial tested Lü Dongbin's honesty. At a market, he bought some bronze utensils. But, when he returned home and polished them, he realized that they had been, in fact, made of gold. Instead of keeping them, he came back to the seller and corrected his mistake.

The eighth trial was that of bravery. One day at a market, Lü Dongbin encountered a Taoist seller who claimed that he was selling magical potions. The man seemed crazy and his potions shady at best. The seller said that it would either kill a man on the spot or it would make him immortal. Unsurprisingly, nobody at the market was willing to test this—apart from Lü Dongbin who drank the potion without fear, and nothing happened to him. It had been a scam, after all.

During the ninth trial, Lü Dongbin was crossing a river with a couple of people on a raft. Suddenly, the weather got worse and heavy rain started falling. The people who were traveling with Lü despaired and feared death, but Lü showed no fear. They all crossed safely to the other shore.

And finally, the tenth trial happened when Lü was alone at home. He was going about his chores when, suddenly, odd things started happening. Ghosts started howling in the cracks and crevices, attempting to scare Lü. But he was unperturbed and continued with his duties.

Then, terrifying demons appeared. They had blood all over their figures, and they started saying unimaginable things to Lü—that in his past life, he had killed a demon and, as a result, his life now belonged to them. Lü was still unmoved; demons were prone to deceit, after all. Finally, when the demons didn't stop pestering them, he said that they could go right ahead and claim his life—he was not afraid.

That was when the sky suddenly turned from black to blue and when all the demons disappeared. Only Zhongli Quan was now standing before Lü Dongbin, saying that he had passed the trials and was ready to become an Immortal and a Taoist master along with him. From then on, Lü Dongbin would help many people achieve perfection through Dao.

As an Immortal, Lü Dongbin is often portrayed as less perfect than he was when he was still training to surpass his mortality. He is said to sometimes indulge in drinking too much and to be too quick to passion— meaning both anger and sexual passion. For that reason, people often pray to him for luck in love.

Han Xiangzi

Han Xiangzi is skilled in magical art and playing the flute. He lived during the Tang Dynasty and is believed to have written many poems for imperial occasions. According to one legend, he was a nephew of Han Yu, a famous poet from the Tang Dynasty. In the same legend, Han Yu, who was raising Han Xiangzi after the death of his parents, wanted the boy to pursue worldly matters, while Han Xiangzi wanted to study the ways of Dao.

Han Yu was very unhappy with Han Xiangzi's desires. So he married the young man off to a beautiful woman and a daughter of a scholar, hoping that this would dissuade him from his Taoist dreams.

But Han Xiangzi never consummated the marriage. For a number of years, he kept the pretense of being an exemplary official and a husband, but finally, he ran away, joining Zhongli Quan and Lü Dongbin in their Taoist school. There, after a series of trials, he became immortal.

But he didn't forget about his family. He wanted to grant his uncle and aunt, who had been good parental figures to him, the same immortality that he had been granted. Unfortunately, the couple didn't follow the ways of Dao.

One day, Han Xiangzi left his solitary abode. It was Han Yu's birthday, and he wanted to join in the festivities. But when he appeared at the feast, he had to listen all night long as his uncle tried to convince him to abandon Taoism. Han Xiangzi politely replied that though he was sure his uncle had his best interests at heart, their ways were different. As he was leaving, he left some earth in a flower pot; immediately, a whole bunch of peonies sprung out from it, one of them with a poetic inscription on its petals. The inscription said some cryptic words about the snow in the mountainous Blue Pass and about being unable to travel on (Wu & Yu, 2012).

The explanation of the riddle came years later when Han Yu was demoted from his position as a minister for his criticism of Buddhism; he was an impious man in general, and now, he had been banished for it. He had to travel to a faraway eastern province of Guangdong. But as he was traveling through the Blue Pass, his carriage was snowed in and he couldn't carry on, nor could he turn back. He suddenly remembered Han Xiangzi's prophecy and started crying, realizing the error of his ways.

But that was when Han Xiangzi appeared before him. He miraculously cleared the pass and let him ride on. Out of gratitude, Han Yu started following the ways of Dao. Eventually, both him and his wife would also join the ranks of the Immortals.

Zhang Guolao

During his mortal life, Zhang Guolao was an alchemist who lived during the Tang Dynasty. From the very beginning of his life, he lived as a hermit in the mountains of southwest China, and nobody knew when exactly he was born, as he claimed to be a couple of hundreds years' old and to have been a minister to the legendary Emperor Yao.

Although he was a great ascetic and could refrain from eating for days, Zhang Guolao was very fond of wine. In fact, after he became immortal, he would prepare the wine for all of the Eight Immortals, using his extensive knowledge of herbs. His wine was believed not only to entertain but also to heal. This talent of Zhang was only a part of his rather eccentric nature: He had an affinity for jokes as well as for suddenly vanishing and other magical tricks. He would be, for instance, capable of snatching birds from the sky mid-flight or of traveling on a mule that he would later be able to hide in his pocket. He was also capable of turning himself into a bat—a symbol of immortality and permanence.

During his lifetime, many emperors tried to invite Zhang to their palaces, but he always refused the invitation. Only when the empress Wu Zetian sent him a message, did he agree to come. But he died suddenly on the road, and his body was consumed by worms. This was, however, only a semblance of death; he was later seen in his hermitage as his spirit prevailed and he became immortal, and his tomb was found empty.

Zhongli Quan

Finally, we reach the last of the Eight Immortals— Zhongli Quan, whom we have already mentioned. We know a lot of his life story from the time he was Lü Dongbin's master—but here, let us start from the beginning.

Zhongli Quan was born during the Han Dynasty, in an ancient city of Yanjing. From the very beginning of his life, he showed signs of being destined for greatness: He cried for seven days after he was born, and during his birth, beams of light filled the room where his mother was laboring. He had a broad forehead, long eyebrows, and big ears—all traditional signs of wisdom and greatness.

As Zhongli's father was a courtier, Zhongli followed his example. He entered the emperor's army and became a general. He took part in many battles, among them one against the forces of Tibet.

The Tibetan army beat Zhongli Quan's forces, and the general was forced to retreat into the mountains. As he was fleeing the scene, he stumbled upon an old man. The man offered to show him the way to a sanctuary; Zhongli, fearing about his life and seeking refuge, agreed.

In the sanctuary, the old man taught Zhongli the secrets of alchemy and the ways of Dao for three days. After that intense time, he told him to come back to his homeland and use that knowledge to help people. Zhongli had many questions, the least of which pertained to the identity of the man—but when he turned to speak to him again, the man had already vanished, and the whole sanctuary was gone with him.

Zhongli returned to China. With the help of alchemy and a magical fan the old man had given him, he produced silver and golden coins and saved people from poverty. This continuous practice, in time, transformed him into an Immortal.

Caishen

Caishen is the god of wealth. People often pray to him during the New Year celebrations, asking him for financial help in the upcoming year. His traditional attributes are a golden rod—or an iron rod that is capable of turning everything it touches into gold—and a black tiger, upon whose back Caishen is said to travel. Over the years, multiple attempts have been made to connect Caishen to a historical figure—mostly to court officials or marshals with the affinity for business—but there is no consensus in that regard (*Caishen*, 2019).

Cánshén

Cánshén is the deity of silkworms and silk production and can exist in both female and male form. As a goddess, Cánshén is tied to Hòutǔ, the goddess of the Earth, and can be seen as a wife of the legendary Yellow Emperor—she is worshiped as such mostly in northern and eastern China. As a god, Cánshén is viewed as an ancestor of the Shu people, who first taught them how to use silkworms for silk production. Male Cánshén is mostly worshiped in the Sichuan province in central China.

Chenghuangshen

Chenghuangshen can be interpreted either as an individual god or as a category of deities. He is the god of boundaries who protects any given city, town, or village from external threats. In Chinese folk religion, it is a belief that people from the same location go to one common location after death—and so, Chenghuangshen guards the corresponding location in the afterlife as well. Some local versions of Chenghuangshen might be deified mortals: prominent leaders of cities and towns who began to be worshiped after their death.

In general, an inhabitant of a given settlement can pray to their local Chenghuangshen for everything: individual health; proving one's innocence when accused of a crime; good weather; and protection from bandits, wars, natural disasters, etc. Virtually every settlement would have a temple of Chenghuangshen.

In a way, Chenghuangshen would act very much like a spiritual official. It was believed that he would even conduct censuses of ghosts living in a given place, to account for them all and ensure they didn't want for anything: neither food, drink, nor winter clothing. He would also lead ghost processions on crucial feasts of the year. And like a mortal official, Chenghunagshen would also be held accountable if he failed in his duties: for instance, if he didn't deliver the much sought-for rainfall, his image could be exposed to the sunrays or be whipped by a magistrate (Yang, 1961).

Chen Jinggu

Chen Jinggu is the goddess of women, pregnancy, and childbirth. During her life, she is believed to have been a Taoist priestess who was born around 766 (Sharar & Weller, 1996). She was deified after death for her extraordinary piety.

According to the legend, when she was young, Chen Jinggu ran away from home to escape an arranged marriage and attended a Taoist school at Lushan, in today's Jiangxi province in eastern China. There, she learned all the ways of Dao but not a lot about maternity and pregnancy. Having finished school, she returned to her hometown and married.

As a married woman, she continued to help people in need, using her knowledge of Dao. She would subdue evil spirits and bring rain during the periods of drought. During that time, she also became pregnant.

One day, a terrible drought hit the area of Fujian where Chen Jinggu lived. In order to bring rain to the province, Chen had to battle a snake demon. At first, she tried to use the powers of Dao to vanquish it, but in the end, she had to sacrifice the fetus in her womb and eventually also herself.

The rain came to the province, and the people rejoiced. They started worshiping Chen Jinggu, and eventually, because of her sacrifice, she became the goddess of expecting mothers.

Chen Jinggu's story is fascinating. Not only did she defy traditional gender roles by first escaping an arranged marriage, and then essentially performing an abortion to save her community—but she was also deified for it, and no criticism of her action is to be found. However, she still became a rather traditional goddess of pregnancy and childbirth.

Erlang Shen

Erlang Shen is a god of engineering, responsible especially for regulating floods in China. According to the legends, he is the nephew of the Jade Emperor, the God of Heaven, himself (Wu & Yu, 2012). However, like many other Chinese gods, Erlang Shan started his life as a mortal, a son of an engineer during the Qin Dynasty.

From his earliest years, Erlang assisted his father in many of his irrigation projects. However, there was still a considerable problem with flooding in the area, and so, Earlang's father sent him out into the countryside to investigate the source.

It took Erlang a whole year of futile searching, and he still couldn't find the source of the flood. But one day, as he was taking shelter in a mountain cave, he met a tiger. He killed the wild animal just in time for the seven local hunters to witness the event. Taken by Erlang's bravery, the hunters promised to help him out on his quest.

At last, the newly formed fellowship reached the modern-day outskirts of Dujiangyan City in southwest China, which back then was called Guan. Even from behind the walls of the city, the men could hear wailing. When they entered, they met an old woman who was crying profusely on account of her grandson, who was going to be sacrificed to a local water dragon. Erlang breathed deeply: He had finally found the source of the flood.

Erlang reported back to his father, who set out to devise the dragon's capture plan. Erlang and his seven companions then hid in the dragon's temple. The poor boy was left tied up in the middle of the space, and just as the dragon slithered inside to eat him, the companions jumped out of the shadows and captured him. Then, the old woman chained the dragon up with irons. The boy and the whole city were saved, and the area was now free of flooding.

Huang Daxian

Huang Daxian, or Wong Tai Sin, is the god of healing. Yet again, he started his life as a mortal and is believed to have been born in the 3rd or 4th century (Geertz et al., 2000). He wasn't a member of a prominent family; instead, he was born into poverty, and was forced to become a shepherd when he was only eight. He spent seven years in that trade, until one day, as he was herding sheep on the slopes of the Red Pine Mountain near his hometown, he met an Immortal who started teaching him the ways of Dao. It took Huang Daxian many years to master that craft, but 40 years later, he was so skilled that he could turn stones into sheep. He was also an exceptional healer.

Due to his place of residence, Huang Daxian became known as the Red Pine Immortal.

Jiutian Xuannü

Jiutian Xuannü is the goddess of sex and longevity, on one hand, and of war, on the other. She is believed to have been the tutor of the legendary Yellow Emperor himself. When the emperor was at a conflict with Chiyou, the god of war, she helped him against a thick mist that his opponent had created: She rode into it in a colorful garment and holding phosphorous, radiant reins. She also gifted the Yellow Emperor several magical objects that would help him defeat Chiyou: magic talismans and charts that would allow him to grasp the essence of Yin and Yang and win the battle using them—and other magical martial charts. Because of this, Jiutian Xuannü became the goddess of war.

It is said that Jiutian Xuannü is very skilled in the supernatural art of war. She can make herself and the ones whom she favors invisible with the help of her six maidens, which is connected to the feminine Yin principle, whose nature lies in invisibility (Liu, 2016). She also knows incantations that would allow the caster to engage the stars from the Big Dipper constellation on the caster's side.

As a goddess of longevity, Jiutian Xuannü is an expert on the human body, which, according to Taoism, is a microcosm of the world (Cahill, 2013). The goddess is said to be responsible for the circulation of breath in the human body, thus giving it its necessary vital essence. She is also a master alchemist.

The third area of Jiutian Xuannü's expertise—sexuality—seems slightly haphazard. But there are Taoist texts that connect her to that sphere (Cahill, 2013). Because of her association with prolonging life, knowledge about the human body, and alchemy, the goddess was associated with the knowledge of various sexual activities. Sex is often compared in Taoism to the art of alchemy, which can be dangerous when used incorrectly, and life-giving, if practiced according to the knowledge of the elements (Cahill, 2013). Over time, however, the sexual element of Jiutian Xuannü was purged from her worship, only to leave way for the martial element.

Lu Ban

Lu Ban not only started his life as a mortal, but he was an attested historical figure. He was born ca. 507 B.C.E. and died in 444 B.C.E., during the Zhou Dynasty, and was a carpenter, engineer, and inventor (Yan, 2010). He is believed to have invented, among others, tools such as the saw, grappling hooks, and a ram important for naval warfare, as well as a prototype of a kite (Yan, 2010).

After his death, Lu Ban started to be revered as the god of carpentry and masonry. Sometimes, he is also worshiped as a water deity, as his inventions are believed to provide for a safe naval journey.

Tu'er Shen

Tu'er Shen is an unusual god: He is specifically responsible for love between men. He was mostly revered in Fujian, where the story of his mortal life was said to take place.

The story of Tu'er Shen was written down in a collection of supernatural stories in 1788, but the story and the cult itself are definitely older (Szonyi, 1998).

According to the tale, the god used to be a mortal man named Hu Tianbao, who lived in the Fujian province. One day, he saw an inspector of the province. The man was very handsome, and Hu immediately fell in love with him. He was so obsessed that he sneaked up to the inspector's home and peeped at him through a hole in a bathroom wall.

Unfortunately for Hu, he was caught. Asked what he was doing, he revealed his affection for the inspector. Furious, the official sentenced Hu to death by beating. And that would be the sad end of Hu Tianbao's life, if it weren't for the gods.

A month after Hu's death, a man from his village had a dream. In this dream, Hu appeared in a form of a rabbit and told him that the gods of the underworld decided to be merciful for him: Because his crime sprung out of love, they decided to make him a god of homosexual relations and to keep safe those who were in a similar position to him. Prompted by the dream, the villagers built a temple to Hu, who from that point on was called Tu'er Shen. The rabbit became a symbol of homosexuality.

The folk cult of Tu'er Shen was problematic for the Chinese government. At around the same time when Hu Tianbao's story was written down, attempts were made by Fujian officials to suppress the cult, and the depiction of Tu'er Shen embracing another man was found "licentious" (Szonyi, 1998). Over the 19th and 20th century, the cult was partly suppressed, partly forgotten. It was only in 2006 when Lu Wei-ming, a Taoist priest from Taiwan, erected a new temple of Tu'er Shen in New Taipei City (Gold, 2015). Today, thousands of people visit the temple every year, and its priests also perform gay marriage ceremonies.

Zao Shen

Zao Shen, also known as the Kitchen God or the Stove God, is the protector god of the hearth and of family and one of the most important gods connected to the domestic sphere. He is believed to have been a mortal before attaining divinity. There are different versions relating how this happened, but the most popular one identifies him as a man named Zhang Lang who lived in the 2nd century B.C.E. (Wolf & Martin, 1978).

Zhang Lang was a relatively ordinary man whose life didn't have anything unusual about it. He grew up and married a respectable woman. But that was when his good life decisions ended. He soon met a younger, more beautiful woman and left his wife for her.

The gods didn't like Zhang Lang's conduct. For abandoning his wife, they struck him with blindness. Soon, his new young lover, who was far less virtuous than Zhang's wife, didn't find him that alluring anymore. She abandoned him and left him to fend for himself, even though it was extremely difficult to do so with his new disability.

Zhang Lang was forced to become a beggar. He would wander from street to street, asking for alms. But one day, he happened to walk past the area where his and his former wife's house stood; just as he did, his wife walked out of the house. Not recognizing her because of his blindness, Zhang extended his hand, asking for some money.

The woman, even after having been treated so poorly, still found compassion in her heart. She told him to come into her house, where she cooked him a generous meal. As he was eating, Zhang, still not realizing who the woman was, started telling his life story to her.

As he was speaking, he became more and more emotional. He now recognized the error of his ways, and he wished more than anything that he could meet his wife and apologize to her. The woman, overcome with emotion, started crying. She then told him to open his eyes.

Zhang did; then, with astonishment, he realized that he could see again. Mortified, he saw his former wife sitting before him. She had not only taken pity on him, but she had been more than generous. Shamed, Zhang Lang jumped up and threw himself into the kitchen hearth. The flames consumed his body instantly, and even though his wife tried to save him, she only managed to pull one of his legs from the fire.

She then created a shrine to the memory of her husband and put it above the fireplace. Thus, the cult of Zao Shen started.

There are many traditions connected to the worship of Zao Shen. It is believed that he watches over everything that is going on in a given household and reports it to the God of Heaven. Many people in China to this day keep paper effigies of Zao Shen and his wife and smear their heads with honey so that the god's reports about the deeds of the family members might be presented in a favorable light. The Kitchen God Festival, held on the 23rd day of the 12th lunar month of the Chinese calendar, also known as the "Little New Year," is believed to be the day when Zao Shen brings his report to the God of Heaven (Wolf & Martin, 1978). After that date, the paper effigy of the god is burnt and replaced with a new one.

Gods of Animals and Vegetables

Finally, our journey brings us to the last category of deities described in this chapter—this time ones who are responsible for animals and plants. Because we have already talked about Shennong, one of the Three Sovereigns who is also the god of crops, we will only focus on one other deity whose area of expertise centers around animals.

Húshén

Húshén, or Huxian, is a fox deity—represented as either male or female. He or she can shapeshift into a fox and takes care of both the animals living in the natural world, as well as of the fox spirits—whom we will talk about in the next chapter. The deity is particularly worshiped in northeastern China and Manchuria, where each newborn child receives their own manifestation of Huxian, male for the boys and female for the girls (Kang, 2006). In general, the worship of the fox deity in these regions is overwhelmingly popular.

Chapter 4:

Mythological Creatures

In this chapter, I want to take you for a journey through the versatile world of Chinese supernatural creatures. From symbolic beings, through animals with special properties, to ghosts, spirits, and monsters—Chinese mythology and folklore has a lot to offer.

Four Symbols

The Four Symbols are tied to Chinese astronomy and knowledge about the natural world. Each creature— which might also be known as one of the Four Guardians or Four Auspicious Beasts—is tied to one cardinal direction of the compass and to one of the elements of the *wuxing*, as well as to an emotion, a season, a time of day or night, a color, and a virtue. As stars, they all also possess seven mansions in the sky, corresponding to seven phases of the Moon.

The Four Symbols are at the core of ancient Chinese knowledge about the organization of the world and an art of harmonizing oneself with the environment— known as *feng shui*. In many classifications, they are guarded by a fifth symbol or element—the yellow chimerical creature called Qilin, of whom we will talk later.

Starting from the symbol of the North, the Four Auspicious Beasts are as follows:

North: Black Tortoise

The Black Tortoise of the North corresponds to the season of winter as well as to midnight. His *wuxing* element is water. Portrayed as a tortoise entwined with a snake, he represents longevity and wisdom. He is also known as the Dark Warrior, or the Mysterious Warrior, and could have a dark side.

East: Azure Dragon

The Azure Dragon stands for the East and the spring and the dawn. His *wuxing* element is wood. He is associated with justice, wealth, and good fortune. His azure hue means that he could be represented by both colors green and blue.

The Azure Dragon is often depicted on the doors to Taoist temples and is said to guard them. He can protect cities as well.

South: Vermilion Bird

The Vermilion Bird—a very specific shade of red— guards the South and stands for midday and summer.

His *wuxing* element is fire, and he's the symbol of good luck. He's an elegant bird who slightly resembles a pheasant.

West: White Tiger

Finally, the White Tiger stands for the West, autumn, and dusk. His *wuxing* element is metal. Warfare, power, and courage are the concepts associated with him. He is believed to be a protector against evil spirits.

A possible origin story for the White Tiger might come from a folk belief that a tiger is the king of all animals and that it can live very long, sometimes over 500 years. An ancient tiger like that would have a white tail, and it would only appear in the wild during a time of an absolutely just and virtuous emperor—or during a time when there is no war in the entire world. Both feats were, of course, very difficult to achieve.

Dragons

The famous Chinese dragons, so characteristic and different from the dragons known from the European tradition, are perhaps one of the most iconic elements of Chinese mythology. Their most common form is that of a creature with a fierce mouth, long whiskers, snake-like body, and four legs—but there are also dragons with a body of a turtle or a fish. Contrary to vicious European dragons, the Chinese dragons are considered largely benevolent and auspicious. However, they can also sometimes pose danger, and their might and power became a symbol on its own, used by the Chinese emperors to indicate the power of their station.

As we have already learned from the previous chapters, most dragons are associated with water, guarding seas, rivers, and lakes. They are also said to control the weather.

As mentioned in the section devoted to the divine Dragon King, there are a couple of dragon groupings which are considered either messengers and servants of the Dragon King, or his incarnations. Here, we will talk about the Five Dragon Kings responsible for the five regions in the world and about Four Dragon Kings of four seas.

Five Dragon Kings

The Five Dragon Kings are five chthonic, or underworld, beings, which guard the five regions of the world: North, South, East, West, and Center. They are similar to the Four Symbols in that the colors associated with them are the same; in fact, the Azure Dragon guarding the East is the same creature as the Auspicious Beast from the previous section.

Apart from the Azure Dragon, there are: the Black Dragon of the North; the Red Dragon of the South; the White Dragon of the West; and the Yellow Dragon of the Center. Since ancient times, these dragons have been invoked during rites and prayers for rain.

Four Dragon Kings

The Four Dragon Kings are associated with four "seas" (meaning large bodies of water) that create natural boundaries of China and were regarded in the past as the edges of the known world. These include: Ao Guang of the East China Sea; Ao Run of Qinghai Lake in the west; Ao Qin of the South China Sea; and Ao Shun of Lake Baikal in the north. It is said that the four dragons were sent to the four corners of the world when they started growing up rapidly and became too rowdy for the Dragon King to manage on his own. Out of the four dragons, Ao Guang and Ao Run both have legends associated with them.

A legend connected to Ao Guang was described in the *Journey to the West* (Wu & Yu, 2012) and concerns the relations between Ao Guang and Sun Wukong, the Monkey King.

One day, the Monkey King wished to have a weapon that would befit him. He sought out his advisors who then told him that this kind of weapon could be obtained from Ao Guang, the dragon of the East Sea. So the Monkey King set out on a journey.

When he arrived at Ao Guang's palace, the Dragon King let him try out several weapons. But Sun Wukong was too strong, and each of them broke in his hands. Then, Ao Guang's wife came and suggested trying out Ruyi Jingu Bang. It was a magical weapon: a self-expanding iron staff covered with golden rings. When Sun Wukong approached it, the weapon started glowing, which indicated that it was destined for him.

The Monkey King grabbed the staff which shrank, accommodating itself to his height.

Ao Guang was awed. But unfortunately, the staff had another important role: It regulated the sea tides, so when Sun Wukong took it, the water started whirring and flowing uncontrollably. From that point onwards, its waters became treacherous.

Ao Run, the Dragon King of the West Sea, is another one of the four dragons with a legend tied to him. When the four dragons were sent out to settle in the various seas in the four corners of the world, Ao Run eagerly volunteered to become the dragon of the West Sea. His brothers laughed at him: To their knowledge, the West Sea didn't exist. But they didn't tell this to Ao Run; instead, they sent him on his quest. The bewildered dragon flew over China up to Qilian Mountain in the west but didn't see any body of water. Exhausted, he cried out in distress, realizing that he'd been duped.

He then climbed the peak of Qilian Mountain and created a massive storm. Rain started falling, forming a small lake at the foot of the mountain, but it was not enough for a sea. Ao Run wept.

But his struggles were seen by the God of Heaven. In his mercy, he sent the god of thunder Leishen to aid Ao Run in his work. Leishen created a storm even greater, and all the rain that fell down on that part of the world that day created the massive Qinghai Lake.

Mythological Fish

Fish are an important element of Chinese cultural imagination. They can be either fish found naturally in the environment who have become mythological symbols or particular fish with supernatural powers.

The presence of fish can be used as a way of telling the fortune. For instance, their abundance in rivers has been traditionally interpreted as a sign of good harvest (Eberhard, 2015). In general, they would be viewed as a symbol of good luck and especially wealth. For example, eating fish during the New Year ceremony is supposed to bring prosperity (Eberhard, 2015). In Chinese Buddhism, fish represent deliverance from suffering (Eberhard, 2015).

Goldfish, specifically, are believed to bring gold; they can also be a symbol of fertility (Eberhard, 2015). Carp, on the other hand, are supposed to give people advantage in business negotiations. It is a belief that they can also sometimes turn into dragons.

Magical Snakes

Snakes in Chinese mythology often represent hidden powers: I have already mentioned that the primordial pair of gods, Nüwa and Fuxi, are depicted as humans with snake tails instead of legs. Moreover, snakes can often shapeshift into humans, or they can form hybrids with tortoises, as was the case with the aforementioned Black Tortoise of the North.

Snakes are often guardians of rivers due to their serpentine shape. In the Chinese zodiac, Snake is one of the constellations.

There is one particularly famous legend connected to a shapeshifting snake: *Legend of the White Snake,* which was written down during the Ming Dynasty and which we will now recount in full.

Legend of the White Snake

There was once a boy named Xu Xian. One day, he went to a street vendor who was selling tangyuan—a traditional Chinese rice balls dessert. But the vendor he encountered was no ordinary person—this was one of the Eight Immortals in disguise, Lü Dongbin, and the tangyuan were actually immortality pills. Xu Xiuan ate one of the pills, which caused him to stop feeling hunger for the next three days.

Growing increasingly concerned, Xu Xian went back to the vendor. Lü Dongbin, being of a rather passionate and volatile nature, only laughed and suddenly caught the boy by his waist. He flipped him over, causing him to vomit the rice ball. As they had been standing on a bridge, the ball fell into a lake.

But the lake wasn't unoccupied. A powerful white snake was living in it—a creature capable of shapeshifting, who moreover was studying Taoism in order to attain immortality. The pill now provided it with an easy way of doing so—it immediately prolonged its lifespan by 500 years. Moreover, as this happened thanks to Xu Xian, now the fates of the snake and of the boy were intertwined.

Eighteen years then passed, during which time the white snake attained one friend and one enemy. The enemy was a turtle who was jealous that it was the snake who caught the immortality pill, not him, and the friend was a green snake whom the white snake bought from a vendor, using its shapeshifting powers, and adopted as a sister.

During this time, the white and the green snake wanted to go to a festival. Now, the green snake also possessed shapeshifting powers, and so they both transformed themselves into beautiful maidens: The white snake became a woman called Bai Suzhen, and the green one a girl named Xiaoqing. As it happened, it started raining just as the two women reached the bridge where, all those years ago, Xu Xian vomited the immortality pill, and this time, Xu Xian was also there. Seeing two beautiful women without an umbrella, he immediately walked up to them and offered his assistance. Bai Suzhen fell in love with him on the spot. She knew who he was, but he didn't know her. Not long after, the couple got married and opened a shop with medicines together.

But the turtle didn't spend all those years idly. He directed all his efforts into getting revenge on the white snake. So he studied Taoism and accumulated power, until he, too, could turn into a human. He transformed himself into a Buddhist monk and named himself

Fahai. In that guise, he went to the home of Xu Xian and Bai Suzhen.

Using his perceived authority as a monk, Fahai told Xu Xian that during an upcoming festival, his wife should drink traditional realgar wine; it had the power to turn her back into her snake form. And that is what happened. In the middle of the festivities, unsuspecting Bai Suzhen drank the wine and turned into a snake. Xu Xian, shocked beyond anything he'd experienced in his life, was struck dead on the spot.

But Bai Suzhen couldn't live with this. She took Xiaoqing, and they both traveled to Mount Emei in Sichuan province. There grew special herbs that had the power of restoring people to life. The two snake-sisters gathered the herbs and brought Xu Xian back.

Xu Xian saw what his devoted wife had done: He now knew what she was, but he found it within himself that he still loved her. They resumed their married life as before.

But Fahai didn't want to give up. Again, disguised as a monk, he lured Xu Xian away from his home and then captured him in his temple. Again, both Bai Suzhen and Xiaoqing stormed the temple, trying to get Xu Xian back. Bai Suzhen called on her powers and flooded the temple—unfortunately, she also managed to drown many innocent bystanders in the process.

And still, she didn't manage to get her husband back. Because she was at the time pregnant with Xu Xian's child, her powers were limited. So Xu Xian made his own escape plan and managed to sneak out of the temple, to later reunite with Bai Suzhen in the city of Hangzhou. There, Bai Suzhen gave birth to their son, whom they named Xu Mengjiao.

Still, Fahai pursued them. Using a moment of Bai Suzhen's weakness, he captured her and imprisoned her in Leifeng Pagoda, a tall tower in the southern part of Hangzhou. This time, neither Xu Xian nor Xiaoqing managed to get her out. But Xiaoqiong swore revenge on Fahai and devoted all her future life to gathering more power in order to defeat him.

Years passed. Xu Mengjiao grew up and was now a very promising young man, earning the highest marks during the civil service examinations. At the same time, when he came back from school to visit his father, Xiaoqing was finally ready to free her sister. She confronted and battled Fahai who, in the end, was forced to shrink himself and hide in a crab's stomach—from that day on, crab's stomachs are orange, because Fahai's monk garb was this color.

Bai Suzhen was reunited with her family and everything ended well.

Supernatural Birds

Chinese mythology is full of birds—both real-life birds, with symbolic or supernatural meaning, and mythological ones. Next, we will discuss some examples.

Bi Fang Bird

The Bi Fang bird is a fantastical creature. It is a one-legged, crow-like bird whose sighting is regarded as auspicious. The legendary Yellow Emperor, of whom more in the next chapter, was the keeper of Bi Fang birds.

Cranes

Cranes have a symbolic meaning in Chinese culture. They represent immortality, and sometimes can even be gods in disguise or the means of transport for them. Traditionally, Chinese folklore differentiates between four types of cranes: the white ones, blue ones, yellow ones, and black ones. Out of these four, the black ones can be extremely long-lived—even up to several centuries—and are believed to refrain from all food, and only drink water, after they pass the threshold of 600 years (Perkins, 1999).

Fenghuang

Fenghuang is a very important bird: a queen of all birds. It's a mythological creature, traditionally female, that can sometimes pair up with the male Chinese dragon. It's chimeric, meaning that it is made up of body parts of many different birds, including a golden pheasant, a mandarin duck, a peacock, and a crane. Property-wise, it is a bit similar to a phoenix, in that it is associated with flames.

The Fenghuang's feathers come in five colors, each of which represents one virtue according to Confucianism: black stands for Ren (benevolence and charity); white symbolizes Yi (honesty); red means Zhi (knowledge); green stands for Xin (faithfulness, integrity); and last but not least, yellow symbolizes Li (propriety and politeness) (Do-Dinh, 1969).

The Fenghuang symbolizes virtue and grace. It is said that the bird itself is a composite of two birds: male Feng and female Huang—which represents the symbiosis between the Yin and Yang elements. The images of Fenghuang have often been linked with royalty, and especially with the house of the Emperor. Its connotations to sun and fire can be read as a wish for the imperial line to be just and powerful.

The union between the Fanghuang and the dragon can also be read as a metaphor for marriage. It is a merging of two seemingly incongruous elements that, nonetheless, can form a harmonious whole.

Jingwei

The Jingwei bird was a human once. A daughter of Yan, one of the legendary emperors of China, named Nüwa—not to be confused with the goddess Nüwa— was one day swimming in the Eastern Sea. But she swam too far away from the shore, and as she was trying to come back, her muscles gave way and she drowned. The merciful gods, however, turned her into a bird. Jingwei, traumatized by her experience in the sea, started to carry twigs and pebbles in her beak and drop it to the sea floor—something which she is due to perform till the end of time. Jingwei is a symbol of overcoming tragedy, on one hand, but also of inability to let go of the past hurts, on the other.

Qingniao

The Qingniao are a special category of birds: Blue or green, they play the role of messengers of the goddess of the West, Xiwangmu. They live in the wilderness surrounding Xiwangmu's palace on the top of the mythical Kunlun Mountain, and they are three-legged.

Shangyang

The Shangyang is a bird who can predict rainfall. It is one-legged, and it would dance on its one leg when a heavy rainfall is supposed to come. It is said that Confucius himself witnessed this and that he was able to save the state of Qi during the Zhou Dynasty by building an irrigation system before the rainfall came (Yang et al., 2008).

Three-Legged Crow

The three-legged crow is an important symbol not only in Chinese, but also in other Asian mythologies. In China, it represents the sun and is often depicted on the sun disk.

It is said that in the beginning of time, there were ten suns, and each of them had its own crow. They were all under the protection of the goddess Xihe, who would send out one of the suns into the sky every tenth day. But the crows, instead of fulfilling their duty, would fly down to the Earth and eat special grass of immortality. So Xihe covered their eyes in order to prevent them from straying.

But that meant the crows would sometimes get confused. One day, it led to a disaster: All 10 crows flew out into the sky on the same day. The unbearable heat soon caused the whole world to burn, and only the masterful archery skills of a hero named Houyi saved the universe. He shot all the birds apart from one.

Zhenniao

The Zhenniao are dangerous. They are poisonous birds that, according to legends, live in southern China. They have a purple belly, green feathers, and a scarlet beak. Their favorite food is the heads of vipers—hence their poisonous quality. Their meat is said to be highly toxic and smelly, but it can also kill through the touch of its feathers alone—a fact that has reportedly been used in many assassinations—so much, in fact, that the bird's name became associated with the act of assassination itself (Eskildsen, 2012).

Part-Humans

Chinese mythology abounds in creatures that resemble humans, but are not: ghosts and spirits, vampire-like creatures, shapeshifters, part-human monsters...

Ba Jiao Gui

Ba Jiao Gui is the ghost of a banana tree. It is female and often sits at the foot of the tree in the form of a beautiful crying woman with a baby at her breast. The ghost would often beg people to set them free, and a failure to do so might result in a terrible death.

Baigujing

Baigujing is a terrible flesh-eating demoness. She appears in the novel *Journey to the West* (Wu & Yu, 2012). Her true form is that of a skeleton, but she can also disguise herself as a woman.

In the novel, Baigujing wished to eat the body of Tang Sanzang, the protagonist of the book. So disguised as a village girl, she accosted him and his companions on his journey and offered them fruits that were poisonous. But Tang Sanzang's companion the Monkey King Sun Wukong had supernatural powers and was capable of detecting the demoness under the disguise. Before she was able to pass the men her fruits, Sun Wukong hit Baigujing with his staff. The girl fell down, lifeless.

The Monkey King's companions were furious: He didn't tell them why he struck the poor girl. They now started arguing, and Sun Wukong tried to explain his motives, but Tang Sanzang didn't believe in his sixth sense. Saddened, he buried the seemingly dead girl.

But the demoness wasn't dead. When the travelers were gone, she dug herself out of her grave and followed them. For the second time, she put on a disguise of an old woman and spun a tale in which the village girl from earlier had been her daughter. She wished to instill a feeling of guilt in Tang Sanzang and the others, but again, Sun Wukong saw through her disguise and struck her with his staff. The companions started arguing, accusing the Monkey King of murder. So, again, they buried the woman. And again, she dug herself out of her grave.

For the third time, she returned as an old man, pretending to be the father of the family Sun Wukong had slain. This time, the companions couldn't hide their remorse, and again, only Sun Wukong could see the demoness under the flesh. Baigujing started taunting him, throwing insults that only he could hear. Being of short temper, the Monkey King couldn't bear this and, not caring if his companions killed him for this afterwards, he struck at the demon for the third time. But this time his blows were even stronger, and he managed to kill not only the human shell but the essence of the demoness, revealing her true form—a skeleton.

When Tang Sanzang saw this, he rushed to apologize to Sun Wukong for doubting him. But another one of his companions, who had been jealous of the Monkey

King's powers, convinced Tang Sanzang that it had all been a trick done by Sun Wukong in order to feign his innocence. Tang Sanzang then argued with the Monkey King and banished him from his company. They would only reunite later when Tang Sanzang would be attacked by another demon and would have no choice but to call on Sun Wukong and to put all grievances away.

Chimei

Chimei is a dragon-like mountain demon. He usually lives in dangerous wilderness and torments those who have been banished there. In art, he is represented both as a hideous humanoid monster and as a hornless dragon.

Daolaogui

Another mountain spirit, Daolaogui lives in the Jiangxi Province. His presence can be sensed through the advent of strong wind and heavy rainfall, both of which he uses to hide his inhuman shriek. He can attack people with poisonous gas, and when untreated, this might turn the victims into Daolaogui themselves. There are female and male Daolaogui, and the female ones are slightly less toxic but still deadly.

E Gui

E Gui literally means "hungry ghost" (Teiser, 1996). It is a belief in Buddhism that those who were driven by strong, uncontrolled emotions during life would then turn into E Gui. This is not necessarily an eternal punishment: Eventually, a person's emotions would fade in time and they would die a second time, allowing for the reincarnation of their spirit.

The concept of hungry ghosts became so popular in Chinese Buddhism that it created a separate realm, the World of the Hungry Ghosts. A special festival is held, dedicated to E Gui—the Hungry Ghost Festival during the seventh month of the Chinese lunar calendar. It is a belief that during this month, the gates of the Hungry Ghosts' World are open and they are free to roam the Earth, seeking food and entertainment and sometimes playing tricks. The ghosts have to be placated with food and offerings of comfortable life in the underworld; small paper effigies symbolizing various forms of entertainment (e.g. paper houses, and today, even cars, televisions, or computers) are burnt in order to symbolically provide the ghosts with their comfort. On the 15th day of the month, large feasts are held by the local communities. Each member of the community brings a sample dish which is then laid down for the ghosts to partake in—this is supposed to bring good luck and prevent from possession, which might end up in madness. During the day of the festival, the streets are closed in order to allow the ghosts to roam freely; and in the evening, concerts and various shows are organized. The first couple of rows in the audience are always empty—reserved for the ghosts.

Hiderigami

Hiderigami is a spirit that is common to both Chinese and Japanese folklore, but its story originated in China and is tied to the tale of the god of war Chiyou, from the time when he attacked the Yellow Emperor.

Hiderigami, then called Hanba, used to be a goddess. The Yellow Emperor employed her to attack Chiyou, who had conjured a mighty storm. Hanba was a terrifying sight to behold: She was dressed in black clothes and her head was bald, and blinding light and scorching heat were radiating off her body. Chiyou's storm died out and the Yellow Emperor was able to capture him.

But the price for this achievement was the loss of divine power for Hanba. From then on, she became a restless spirit who would roam the dry northern terrains of China. Wherever she went, she sucked out water from that place.

Heibai Wuchang

The Heibai Wuchang are two spirits of the underworld, responsible for escorting the souls from the realm of the living to the realm of the dead. They are one of two pairs that serve the god of the underworld, the other one being the Ox-Head and Horse-Face, about whom we will talk in a bit.

As many pairs of beings in Chinese mythology, the Heibai Wuchang have opposing characteristics but, nonetheless, complement each other. There is the White Guard who brings just rewards to the righteous, and the Black Guard who punishes the evildoers.

Huapigui

Huapigui was first described during the Qing Dynasty in a novel called *Strange Tales from a Chinese Studio* (Ni, 2018). He is a terrifying ghost—not only does he eat humans, but he also wears their skin, impersonating them. He especially delights in killing young, beautiful women.

Jiangshi

The Jiangshi are perhaps best described as the Chinese versions of vampires. Their description was first provided in the 18th century (Yu & Branscum, 2021). They are best defined as long-dead bodies that, for many reasons, don't decompose but are, instead, possessed by spirits. This can happen at any stage after the corpse becomes lifeless; hence, some Jiangshi look almost like ordinary people, and others are terrifying, with rotting flesh falling off their bodies. All of them, however, possess bodies after the rigor mortis sets in, and so they can't bend their limbs, instead being forced to hop around.

Traditionally, the Jiangshi don't feed on a person's blood but, instead, on their *qi*—the life force. But under the influence of Western writing, tales of bloodsucking Jiangshi also started to appear.

There are several ways in which a victim can escape or fight the Jiangshi. Some of them include: showing the monster its own reflection in a mirror (they are said to be terrified of them); carrying items made of the wood of a peach tree (as the trees of immortality, they have the power to repel evil spirits); or waiting for a rooster's call, as it signifies the arrival of sun which scares the Jiangshi away.

Nü Gui

Nü Gui is a tragic ghost. It's a female spirit of a woman who was wronged during her life—in most versions of the legend, sexually abused—and who committed suicide due to this. During her funeral, she was dressed in red—a sign that her family were hoping that she would come back as a spirit and avenge her wrongs. However, when she became a ghost, she didn't stop with enacting revenge. Instead, she started attacking innocent people, too (mostly men), sucking out their male Yang essence. The red dress became her signature attribute.

Ox-Head and Horse-Face

Another pair of guardians to the underworld, Ox-Head and Horse-Face are hybrid spirits with bodies of men but heads of the respective animals. Usually, they are the first beings that a newly deceased soul meets when they die.

There aren't many legends tied to Ox-Head and Horse-Face, but it is said that the two spirits were created when Yanwang, the king of the underworld, saw a very hard-working ox and a horse nearing the end of their lives, and he decided to reward them for their hard life by making them his servants and messengers.

Pipagui

The Pipagui are one of the most vicious ghosts in Chinese folklore. They typically inhabit humid areas full of poisonous animals, especially insects, and they are responsible for spreading malaria in those places. They can also possess people, causing either malaria or other illnesses that can lead to death.

Shui Gui

The Shui Gui are the ghosts of people who drowned. Since their bodies have decomposed and don't exist anymore, the Shui Gui attack the living close to the places where they had drowned, pull them underwater, and try to possess their bodies. If this goes according to the spirit's wishes, they would return to the land of the living in the victim's body, while the victim would take their place underwater.

Wutou Gui

Wutou Gui are the spirits of decapitated people—either as a punishment or by accident. They are usually harmless, but can be a terrifying sight, as they typically wander around, carrying their own heads in their arms.

You Hun Ye Gui

You Hun Ye Gui is a more general term for ghosts. It can encompass E Gui, as well as other spirits, both vengeful and simply playful. In general, You Hun Ye Gui are all the spirits that have been "lost" in a way that they didn't manage to undergo reincarnation yet. Offerings to those ghosts are made both during the Ghost Festival, as well as throughout the rest of the year. This is to ensure that the restless spirits don't harm people, either through pranks or causing bodily harm.

Yuan Gui

Yuan Gui is another slightly more general term referring to spirits of people who died being wronged in some way. Because of that, they cannot rest but, instead, roam the world seeking to avenge the wrong that was done to them.

Ying Ling

Ying Ling are the spirits of fetuses who never got the chance to be born. Most likely, the idea of such ghosts originated in Japan and was adopted in China.

Zhi Ren

Zhi Ren are spirits that are created rather than emerge spontaneously. They can be made when a paper doll is burnt as an offering to a dead person, and they then become their servants. Typically, every deceased receives a pair of these dolls, one male and one female. They can act as the links between the realms of the living and the dead, becoming messengers of the dead.

Zhong Yin Shen

Zhong Yin Shen is another general term for a spirit that has already left the deceased's body but wasn't reincarnated yet. In Buddhism, this period of time is called Bardo, and typically lasts 49 days (Lama Lodu, 2011). It is undergone by every spirit, so becoming Zhong Yin Shen is a natural state.

Other Animal Spirits

Bai Ze

The Bai Ze is a mythical beast capable of thinking, speaking, and understanding the thoughts and feelings of people. It can have either the body of a cat or of a cow and is often portrayed with a human head, which nonetheless has horns. It is said that it only appeared in

China during the rule of an exceptionally virtuous emperor.

Huli Jing

Huli Jing is a fox spirit, one of the servants of the fox god Húshén, and capable of shapeshifting into a human form and back. As a fox, it looks like an ordinary animal, except it has nine tails instead of one. As a species, Huli Jing are neither good nor bad: They can play either a good or an evil role in stories they appear in. Sometimes, they are interpreted as a good omen, other times, as a monster that needs to be extinguished.

In their human form, the Huli Jing often appear as beautiful women, or they can possess women's bodies. In one story, a semi-historical figure, Daji, a consort of one of the kings from the Shang Dynasty, was possessed by a Huli Jing as a punishment for the king's cruelty.

Nian

Nian is a beast that lives underwater, slightly similar to a dragon and a lion. It is especially tied to the Chinese New Year, as it is believed that it emerges from its hideout around this time of year. It would usually feed on animals or people, especially children. Fortunately though, Nian is afraid of the color red—hence, lighting up red lanterns can repel it.

Today, the large puppet of Nian is one of the crucial parts of the New Year celebrations, often being carried around by dancers and accompanied by red lanterns and firecrackers. The symbolic dance serves as a representation of taming the creature.

Panhu

Panhu was a hybrid creature—half-dog, half-dragon. His origin story is quite peculiar: He grew from a golden worm that had been extracted by a royal physician from the ear of an old woman. He then became something of a palace pet—until a threat arose, and the king begged his warriors to bring him the head of his enemy. He even offered his daughter's hand in exchange for that accomplishment.

But none of the king's warriors managed to deliver the head apart from Panhu. When it happened, the king was upset: He had made a promise, and now he had to marry his daughter to a hybrid monster. But Panhu was then miraculously transformed into a handsome young man, and the wedding was a happy affair. Panhu and the princess had six sons and six daughters, all of whom became prominent heroes.

Erlang's Dog

We have met Erlang Shen in the previous chapter of this book. The god of engineering is sometimes portrayed as a mightier figure—an extinguisher of evil spirits. In this guise, he always appears with a faithful dog as his companion, who aids him in his task. The dog is often described as a "celestial dog", which might suggest his ties to the Dog constellation (Burham, 2015).

Longma

Another hybrid creature, Longma is a horse covered with dragon scales, and it is yet another of those animals that can only be spotted when the ruler of the land shows signs of extraordinary virtue. In a way, Longma combines two creatures that were considered the noblest in classic Chinese literature: horses and dragons. There are no stories tied to the Longma, but its purported sighting was reported numerous times in various mythological texts of ancient China.

Luduan

Luduan is another auspicious, hybrid-like creature. It is a deer with a horse's tail and a horn on its head. Its face resembles that of a lion or a dragon. It is a highly skilled and intelligent creature. It can travel thousands of miles in one day and speaks all the languages of the world.

Monkey King

Finally, we reach Sun Wukong, the Monkey King who already appeared numerous times in our stories. He is one of the most popular characters in Chinese folklore, to the point that including him in a story, even if in an episodic role, would elevate the rank of the said story. But who was he in the beginning? How did he happen to become so famous?

The origin story of the Monkey King is described in the *Journey to the West* (Wu & Yu, 2012). Once there was a stone on top of a mythical mountain. Because of its location, the stone was receiving both the Yang energy from Heaven as well as the Yin energy from the Earth. It was out of this stone that Sun Wukong was born. In the beginning, he was an animated monkey made of stone, with glowing gemstone eyes. The light shining from the monkey's eyes was so bright, in fact, that it alerted the God of Heaven himself. But when he investigated the matter, he concluded that the monkey posed no threat.

Meanwhile, Sun Wukong was growing up. He joined a group of ordinary monkeys and spent his time with them. But one day, a task presented itself to him: The monkeys wanted to find a source of a stream in which they were bathing every day. They even declared that whoever did it would become their king. Sun Wukong saw his chance.

He followed the river upstream until he found a large waterfall. Being the only one brave enough to jump through it, he discovered a cave behind it and made it into a new home for the monkeys. Thanks to this, he became their king.

But the prosperity didn't last. As time passed, some of the monkeys from the tribe were growing old and dying—a fact that upset Sun Wukong greatly. So he set out a new goal for himself: to find the source of immortality.

We already know this part of the story, in which Sun Wukong persuaded King Yan, the ruler of the underworld, to wipe out his name from the Book of Life and Death. The Monkey King had many adventures along the way to the underworld and back—but his return home proved to be less triumphant than he had thought.

Immediately upon his return, he learned that a demon had been imprisoning his monkeys and forcing them into slavery. Sun Wukong had to defeat the demon in order to bring peace into his kingdom again. Then, he decided to choose a supernatural weapon for himself:. For this purpose, he went to Ao Guang, the Dragon King of the East Sea, in a story that we have already learned as well. Now that he had such an extraordinary staff and his fame was growing far and wide, Sun Wukong could ally himself with several demon and spirit kings.

At this point, the God of Heaven finally realized that Sun Wukong was more powerful than he had imagined. He invited the Monkey King to Heaven in hopes of keeping him under control and tempering his ambitions. Sun Wukong, unaware of this intent, accepted the invitation with glee.

It was only upon his arrival that he learned he was going to be effectively made the gods' stableboy. It was the lowest possible position, and Sun Wukong was furious. So, on the first day of his job, he set the celestial horses free from their stables and let them wreak havoc in Heaven while he came back to the Earth and proclaimed himself Heaven's equal.

The God of Heaven, furious at this, was close to invading Sun Wukong's kingdom but stopped at the last minute. It would be terribly embarrassing if he failed in subduing some monkey. So he reluctantly agreed for Sun Wukong to keep his terribly pompous title and invited him to Heaven again. This time, he was hoping that keeping the Monkey King as a harmless pampered pet might be the end of all trouble.

So another invitation was issued: This time, Sun Wukong was to be the guardian of the peaches of immortality. As he loved peaches, he accepted. But he soon realized that he was still being omitted in invitations to divine banquets and was, overall, not treated seriously. So he stole and ate the peaches of immortality and came back to his kingdom again.

This time, there was no peaceful solution. The God of Heaven invaded Sun's kingdom, but the Monkey King defeated the heavenly army. A number of deities were sent to placate with him but to no avail. Finally, Erlang Shen was sent to wrestle with him, and it was a terrible sight to behold. Both warriors were evenly matched and made for figures so fearsome that Sun Wukong's army ran away in terror. The Monkey King, embarrassed by this, shapeshifted into a fish and then into a number of other creatures, in order to escape Erlang. In the end, another deity had to distract him in order for Erlang to catch and bind him.

Sun Wukong was now a prisoner of Heaven. The gods put him into a large cauldron filled with burning, poisonous liquid. It was supposed to be a torturous execution aimed at distilling and regaining the peaches of immortality from the Monkey King's body. But when the gods opened the cauldron after 49 days, Sun Wukong jumped out unscathed. The burning liquid fortified his body instead of destroying it.

Sun Wukong had to remain a prisoner, then. He even proposed to become the new God of Heaven, and so he had to spend hundreds of years in prison in order to learn humility. It was only after this time that he was released on parole in exchange for a promise to protect Tang Sanzang, the main character of the *Journey to the West*, on his travel to India. Yet again, we already know about some events of that journey and how Sun Wukong defeated the evil demoness who wanted to consume Tang Sanzang's body.

We don't know a lot of what happened to Sun Wukong after he successfully escorted Tang Sanzang on his quest. The Monkey King is immortal and one of the most powerful creatures in the universe—and so, presumably, he is still alive and ruling his monkey kingdom. Sun Wukong is a fascinating example of a character who is both powerful and slightly ridiculous, who boasts too much and is too quick to anger, but he has credentials to prove his extraordinary prowess. It's a story of how a seemingly harmless monkey can sometimes threaten the order of the universe itself.

Pixiu

Pixiu is another one of hybrid creatures, and one of the more ancient ones—its existence was described as early as the Han Dynasty. It is a winged lion who protects the practitioners of feng shui. Moreover, it is said to bring wealth to those whom it protects, as it is actually said to consume gold and jewels.

Pixiu has a male and a female variant. The males have one antler and specialize in searching for gold. When they find it, they guard it fiercely. The females, on the other hand, have two antlers, and they mostly protect their protegees from evil spirits.

Qilin

Qilin, or Kirin, is perhaps the most illustrious and well-known auspicious chimera. It is a golden, dragon-like creature with horse's hooves which appears during the reign of a virtuous ruler. It can also foretell the arrival of an exceptional sage: A legend says that a Qilin appeared at the time of Confucius' birth (*Qilin*, 1998).

Qilin is also the chief and the guardian of the Four Auspicious Beasts. As they represent four cardinal directions, it stands for the center from which everything stems.

Tianma

Tianma is a winged horse, and a personification of one of the heavenly constellations. It was especially venerated and often depicted during the Han Dynasty.

Xiezhi

Lastly, Xiezhi is an ox-like figure with a leonine head and a long horn on its forehead. It's ferocious-looking, with thick black fur covering its body and with burning eyes. It's not only intelligent but also very wise; it has an extraordinary ability of distinguishing between right and wrong. According to the legend, Shun, one of the mythical Chinese emperors, employed Xiezhi to assist him in court proceedings and to establish the guilt or innocence of suspects (Karlgren, 1946). If the accused was guilty of a crime, Xiezhi would ram them to death with its horn.

Because of this legend, Xiezhi became a symbol of justice throughout many dynasties in China. During the Ming and Qing dynasty, the image of the beast found its way to the badge of office of imperial supervisors.

Chapter 5:

The Age of Heroes

Who Is a Culture Hero?

The line between a hero and a god in Chinese mythology is rather blurry. As we have seen in the previous chapters, many Chinese gods used to be mortals and could be classified as heroes during their earthly life. Similarly, many characters described in this chapter could be classified as gods. However, in this section of the book, I would like to acquaint you with a specific type of heroes: culture heroes, or heroes who introduced important civilizational achievements to society—as well as the first mythical rulers of China. This chapter will be all about origins.

Culture Heroes

Hou Ji

Hou Ji is a legendary figure from the Xia Dynasty. He is credited with introducing millet to humanity—a crucial element of the Chinese nutrition list, especially before wheat was used.

The story of Hou Ji's conception and birth is supernatural. His mother, Jiang Yuan, was a wife of Ku, one of the legendary emperors. Unfortunately, she was barren, but after she once accidentally stepped on a footprint left on the Earth by the God of Heaven himself, she conceived a son.

But Jiang Yuan was an inattentive mother. After Hou Ji was born, she abandoned him several times: in a street, in a forest, and on ice. The reason for this isn't known, but each time, the child was miraculously saved. When Hou Ji grew up, he became the new ruler and introduced millet from northern China. He is believed to be the progenitor of the Zhou Dynasty.

Ling Lun and Kui

Both Ling Lun and Kui are credited with inventing music and dancing and introducing it to China. Ling Lun is said to have lived during the legendary times of the Yellow Emperor and to have worked on flutes made out of bamboo sticks. Those flutes could imitate any bird in existence, both natural and supernatural, and their sound was so pitch-perfect that the emperor ordered all bells in the empire to be attuned to them.

Kui, for his part, was the minister of music to the legendary Emperor Shun. He taught music to the emperor's sons and brought harmony to the universe by the invention of many musical instruments. Drums, especially, were supposed to have been his idea: He defeated monsters and stretched their skins over jars when he created them.

Cangjie

Cangjie, the legendary historian of the Yellow Emperor, is credited with the invention of Chinese characters. The legend says that before the invention of writing, information was conveyed through decorative knots—but the emperor grew tired of it and tasked Cangjie with finding another way.

So Cangjie set out to work, but this soon proved more difficult than he imagined. Sitting on a riverbank, he kept pondering, but couldn't come up with a good idea for even one character.

But as he sat there, suddenly, a Fenghuang flew above his head. The bird was carrying something, and it dropped it right under Cangjie's feet. It was a hoof, but it didn't seem to belong to any horse or other hoofed animal. Cangjie went to a local hunter to ask him about this, and the man explained that this was a hoof of the hybrid creature Pixiu. He pointed out all the differences that separated this particular hoof from that of any other animal.

The conversation proved to be a massive source of inspiration for Cangjie: He now knew that he had to invent unique characters which would capture the essential differences between everything that could be found on Earth. His task now was to observe all things in the universe and learn about their characteristics. After years of study, he managed to come up with a complete list of characters.

The Yellow Emperor showered Cangjie with honors and set out on a task of teaching the new script to his court, ministers, and governors of all provinces. He also ordered Cangjie's monument to be erected on the riverbank where he had been first struck by inspiration.

Three Sovereigns and Five Emperors

Three Sovereigns

We won't talk in detail about the Three Sovereigns here, as we know them already—the gods Fuxi, Nüwa, and Shennong. They are regarded as the first rulers of the world after its creation, and they all significantly improved the life of the people on Earth. After their time was gone, the rule fell to lesser heroes, who were still, nonetheless, exceptional sages—known as the Five Emperors.

Five Emperors

There are numerous lists of Five Emperors in ancient Chinese sources, and many of them contradict each other. For this reason, here I will present you with six figures of whose legendary lives we have the most information.

Yellow Emperor

The Yellow Emperor, already known to us from many other stories, is the most famous of the legendary emperors. He is also known under the name Huangdi, and his mythical reign was supposed to have occurred around 2500 B.C.E. (Fowler, 2005). He was the first ruler to centralize the country, and in fact, the color yellow associated with him often symbolizes the center of the universe.

Before he became the emperor, though, Huangdi lived as a farmer near the city of Qufu in eastern China. He proved his courage even then, taming several wild beasts: two bears, a tiger, and a Pixiu. For these achievements, he became the leader of his tribe, which, at the time, still led a semi-nomadic life. Huangdi then taught his people how to build proper shelters, as well as carts and boats; he even taught people how to produce clothing and grow crops.

As his fame grew, Huangdi was given the rule over bigger and bigger amounts of land. He continued with his inventions: He created bow slings, laid down foundations for the principles of Chinese astronomy and mathematics, and created the first version of a calendar. He tasked Cangjie with creating the Chinese script, and he met with the creature Bai Ze to gain knowledge of all things supernatural. He also created the first diadem and a throne room—both of which would soon serve him as he became the first emperor of China.

But his rule was not without conflict. The Yellow Emperor fought a number of battles. He intervened when a ruler of the neighboring tribes, known as the Yan Emperor, was unable to control the warring warlords within his kingdom. One of the battles Huangdi fought on behalf of Yan was the one with Chiyou, which we have already described in Chapter 3: the Battle of Zhoulou.

After defeating Chiyou, the Yellow Emperor took to neutralizing his rival. He defeated the Yan Emperor in the Battle of Banquan and took over the rule of his domain, establishing himself as the sole ruler of China.

According to the legend, the Yellow Emperor lived for a hundred years (Unschuld et al., 2011). After that time, he sighted a Fenghuang and a Qilin, which both signified his perfect virtue. He was now content with the state in which he left his empire—he could die in peace.

Unsurprisingly, the Yellow Emperor was deified after death. His cult as the ancestor of all Chinese imperial dynasties and as the center of the universe was crucial to China throughout its imperial history. Even after the overthrowing of imperial rule, Huangdi was—and still is—revered as a symbolic father of all people of China, even if his religious cult was banned.

Shaohao

Shaohao, or Jin Tian, was the son of the Yellow Emperor. He ruled China from the ancient city of Qufu for over 80 years. Another version of the legend, however, claims that the Yellow Emperor was his great uncle and that Shaohao was instead conceived from a union of a minor weaver goddess with the planet Venus.

Not much is known about Shaohao's rule, except for its longevity.

Zhuanxu

Zhuanxu is believed to have been a grandson of the Yellow Emperor. Shaohao was his uncle, and even from an early age, Zhuanxu showed much more inclination for rule than Shaohao ever had. He became Shaohao's assistant at the age of 10 and started independent rule at the age of 20.

Zhuanxu is credited with perfecting many inventions of his grandfather: He further developed the calendar and astronomy and unified religion, abolishing some shamanistic practices. Instead, he established a new practice: the sacrifice to the gods of soil and grain, which was performed in China for centuries, right until the end of the Qing Dynasty (Theobald, 2018).

Zhuanxu also made some reforms in the domestic sphere. He is said to have pushed for patriarchal rule over the matriarchal one and to have forbidden incestuous marriages.

Emperor Ku

Ku was Shaohao's grandson and the cousin of Zhuanxu. He was the first one to officially take on the title of an emperor, even though that title had been posthumously ascribed to his predecessors as well. According to the legend, Ku took on a habit of patrolling his kingdom every season: In spring and summer, he would ride a dragon and, in autumn and winter, a horse.

He was a great patron of the arts. He is said to have invented several musical instruments as well as composed songs and created dances with the presence of the Fenghuang birds.

Emperor Ku had many wives, who gave him multiple sons. One of them, Yao, would rule the empire straight after him, but all of them would eventually become rulers, or at least illustrious people. It is said that the culture hero Hou Ji was also one of his sons.

Emperor Yao

Emperor Yao is believed to have ruled for over 70 years, and his reign was marked by a cataclysm. The Yellow River and the River Yangtze flooded, overflowing a vast majority of Yao's territory—an event which later became known as the Chinese version of the Great Flood myth (Yang et al., 2008).

In vain, Yao tried to control the flood. All of the proposals put forth by his advisors didn't work out. Finally, they proposed to send for Yao's distant relative, Shun, as he was said to be wise and competent.

Yao created a series of trials for Shun, testing his prowess. He had to face severe winds, rain, and thunder. He passed all the tests and was allowed to marry two of Yao's daughters and to rule with him as a co-emperor.

Shun

Shun, though in many classifications he doesn't figure on the lists of the Five Emperors, is, nonetheless, important to our story. As we have just witnessed, only his shrewdness and courage helped to put the Great Flood under control. Shun conducted a series of reforms that addressed the immediate crises—such as deepening the overflowing rivers—and perfected the running of the empire overall. It took him three years to put the affairs under order.

But before he became an emperor, Shun had a difficult childhood. Raised by a neglectful stepmother and a stern father, he was never appreciated and always forced to work very hard for very little reward. But he never complained and always showed his compassionate nature. At some point, his stepmother threw him out of his family home, and he was forced to provide for himself. Yet, his natural kindness and talents soon drew people to him. He perfected people's skills everywhere he went: He taught fishermen better fishing practices and showed how to make beautiful pots to the potters. It is no wonder that his fame soon spread far and wide.

As an emperor, Shun is credited to have dealt with a number of supernatural threats: He defeated and banished several foes, including a sea monster and a rival warlord of superhuman strength. It is said that even as an emperor, Shun refrained from enjoying the riches that came with the job and still worked in the fields like a humble farmer. His two wives, who had previously been unused to this simple lifestyle, were, nonetheless, so impressed with their husband that they adapted to it.

But Shun's stepmother and his cruel half-brother, when they learned that Shun had become an emperor, grew extremely jealous. Several times, they conspired to kill him, but Shun managed to escape them thanks to his wisdom. And every time, he showed forgiveness to them until they finally repented.

It is said that Shun died when a sudden illness took him during one of his tours of the country. His wives wept for days over his body, and their tears turned to blood, spotting the bamboo sticks near the place of his death—that is the origin of the spotted bamboo species.

The successor of Shun was Yu, the founder of the Xia Dynasty. His reign started the more official historiography of China.

Chapter 6:

The World of Tales

Eighteen Warriors

The Eighteen Warriors is a ranking of heroes who lived during the Sui and Tang Dynasties based on their skill in martial arts. Some of them are based on historical figures, others were invented in folk stories. They are all described in a classic Chinese novel named *Shuo Tang* (Huang, 2006).

About some of the warriors, not much is known apart from their names, but others earned their place in the corpus of folk tales. In this chapter, I have selected tales about several of the most powerful warriors from the list.

Let's start with Li Yuanba, the most powerful of all heroes. He was the fourth son of Emperor Gaozu (566–635), the founder of the Tang Dynasty. His strength was legendary: He could wield golden hammers, which weighed over 200 kgs each. With these weapons, he defeated the Turks who attacked China at the time.

It is said that one day Li Yuanba was surprised by a sudden and violent thunderstorm. Angry at Heaven for this, he threw his hammers into the sky. But the god of thunder threw his hammer back at him, pinning him to the ground. That is how Li Yuanba died.

The second strongest warrior was Yuwen Chengdu. He came in second only because he was defeated and killed by Li Yuanba, who then took his weapons. Although a hero, he would sometimes be influenced by his family, who were rebels against the Sui Dynasty.

Third came Pei Yuanqing. His weapon of choice was less impressive than Li Yuanba but still quite extraordinary by human standards: a pair of silver hammers, weighing 150 kgs each. He defeated a number of warriors but died when his family was framed for treason and besieged in their fort.

Xiong Kuohai, the fourth warrior on the list, fought with a pair of axes. He was a bit of an anti-hero: A bandit who conducted business through robbery, he, nonetheless, had a strong sense of justice and always helped the poor. Even though he almost got persuaded to join the emperor's troops at some point, he ended up returning to his illegal life when he saw the cruelties some of the generals were capable of. He rebelled against Ma Shumou, a cruel cannibal general who stole children only to eat them. He killed the general, but that was only the beginning.

At some point, Xiong's rebellion almost overthrew the emperor himself. But the emperor set out a trap for all rebellious warriors He organized a martial arts contest in the city of Yangzhou, counting on attracting numerous problematic heroes. His plan was to let them kill each other in the contest and then to trap the rest of them, barring the city gates and killing them all.

But Xiong learned about the emperor's plan. He rushed to the city to warn his friends and companions. As he did so, the gates started closing. Xiong ran to the gate and, using his exceptional strength, held it long enough to allow the people to escape. Then, he died, crushed by the gate.

Many more warriors populate the list of heroes: Some of them fought on the side of the emperor, some were rebels. It is interesting to see both sides of that historical conflict recognized as heroic figures.

Beauty and Pock Face

Did you know that one of the oldest versions of the *Cinderella* story originated in China? *Beauty and Pock Face* is a folk tale that tells a story of a young girl persecuted by her stepmother.

Once upon a time, there was a man. He had two wives, and each of them gave him a daughter. The daughter of the first wife was beautiful, while the second daughter had a face scarred by pox marks. Unfortunately, the man's first wife died in childbirth. The second wife, jealous of the beauty of her stepdaughter, was cruel to her and forced her into the role of a household servant.

But Beauty's dead mother came back, reincarnated into a yellow cow. She helped her daughter with the daily tasks. Soon, however, the stepmother found this out and had the cow killed. Beauty lamented the second loss of her mother. When there was nothing left of the cow but the bones, she collected them into a pot and hid them.

One day, there was a lavish festival in the town. The stepmother took her daughter, Pock Face, but refused to take Beauty with her. Beauty, exhausted by years of cruel treatment, snapped: When the two women were gone, she smashed everything in the house and even, in her rage, destroyed the pot with the yellow cow's bones.

But what was her surprise when from the cracked pot, there came out a horse carrying a beautiful dress and a pair of lovely shoes! Beauty could now dress up and ride the horse to the festival.

But on her way, she lost one of her shoes, which fell into a ditch. Not wanting to soil her dress, she asked some men passing by to retrieve the shoe for her. Each of them agreed but on one condition: that she would marry one of them. She refused to marry a fishmonger, an oil trader, and even a rich merchant, but then a handsome scholar came by and retrieved the shoe for her. She agreed to marry him immediately.

Her family was, understandably, not happy with that turn of events. Beauty's stepmother was especially angry. So when three days after the wedding, Beauty visited her family home out of custom, she made her daughter, Pock Face, push Beauty down a well. The poor girl died, and her murderer then sent word to the scholar, pretending that Beauty had contracted smallpox and couldn't come home just yet. She then wrote a couple of more notes, asking the scholar to send her several precious objects on behalf of her sister.

At last, the scholar got suspicious. So the stepmother came up with another ruse. She sent Pock Face to him, lying that this was really Beauty but that her face had been disfigured by smallpox.

However, Beauty came back from the dead in the body of a little sparrow. Then, the torment of Pock Face began: The bird started taunting her, so she had it killed. But from the spot where she buried the sparrow, a bamboo rose; the scholar used the shoots for meals—to him, they tasted delicious, but Pock Face got ulcers on her tongue. Then, a bed was made out of the bamboo sticks. For the scholar, it was the most comfortable bed in the world, but Pock Face couldn't sleep in it, so she threw it away.

An old, poor woman found the bed and took it home. From then on, her household was blessed since Beauty's spirit did the household chores for her. One day, she found out about this and, with the help of a couple of magical ingredients, helped Beauty come back to life in the flesh.

Beauty then went to the scholar's house and announced herself as his real wife. A series of tests was made in order to determine who really was his wife. Both Beauty and Pock Face walked on eggshells. Beauty didn't break them, while Pock Face destroyed them all. They climbed a ladder made out of knives, and Beauty didn't cut herself even once. Finally, they both jumped into a vat with boiling oil. Pock Face died in agony, while Beauty emerged unscathed.

Pock Face's bones were sent back to her mother who, realizing what had happened, died on the spot. Beauty was avenged and lived with the scholar happily ever after.

The King of Snakes

The King of Snakes is a story of a girl marrying a shapeshifting serpent—much like Xu Xian did in our tale from Chapter 4. The story begins in a snake kingdom, whose ruler, wishing to improve his subjects' status on Earth, found a way to shapeshift into a human. He then found a small but beautiful realm full of blooming flowers and settled there.

One day, an old man was plucking flowers from the Snake Prince's garden. The prince confronted him. The man said that he was only gathering flowers for his daughters: His fourth one was especially beautiful. The prince, intrigued by this, asked him to send the fourth daughter to him the next day. He wished to marry her; if she refused, he would send an army of snakes to devour the old man and his daughters.

Terrified, the man went back home and related the matter to his daughter. The prince wanted a bride; one of the daughters had to sacrifice herself. Unsurprisingly, the fourth and the most beautiful daughter was also the most devoted to her father. She offered to go. A guarding spirit was accompanying her for protection.

In the beginning, everything went well. When the father came to visit his daughter some days after her wedding, she was living in a grand palace and was very happy.

The older daughters, when they heard of this, grew jealous. One of them quickly went to visit her sister, having heard that her husband was away on some business. She asked her sister to show her around her palace and, distracting her, she pushed her down the well.

This was followed by a sequence very similar to that known from the *Beauty and Pock Face*: A bird representing the young sister's spirit flew out of the well, singing the whole truth. At this, the older sister snapped its neck. Then, a bamboo grew out of the spot where the bird was buried, but the older girl chopped it down. The Snake Prince's servants made a chair out of it. When the prince came back home and asked for his wife, the older sister lied, saying that she didn't know where she was. However, the chair came back to life and told the whole story. The wicked sister was executed for murder.

The Magic Lotus Lantern

The Magic Lotus Lantern is a story of an impossible love between an Immortal and a human being. Sanshengmu was a sister of Erlang Shen and a guardian of magical lotus lanterns. One day, she spotted a very handsome man on Earth, and she wished to marry him. However, her brother was against the match.

Sanshengmu then stole one of the lanterns from his palace and went to the Earth. The lantern had a power of stunning and persuasion so that whoever looked into it, might be convinced into following the caster's schemes.

Sanshengmu married the mortal man, and they had a son together. It took Erlang Shen years to localize the couple, but he finally managed to do so when he followed the glow of the lantern. He then kidnapped the little boy and forced Sanshengmu to return the lantern. When she did, he gave up the young boy but captured her instead.

The boy grew up into a young man. He learned about his mother's imprisonment and set out for a journey to regain the magic lantern. He wandered the Earth and encountered many perils. He even stumbled upon the Monkey King who, taken by his bravery, gave him a magical ax.

Finally, the young man found Erlang Shen on the top of a tall mountain. He was standing in front of the magic lantern, ready to fight. The boy lifted his ax; the duel began. Erlang Shen was close to killing the hero, but in the last moment, the light from the lantern penetrated the boy's body, merging with it; thus, he defeated the god.

He now had supernatural power. He struck the mountain with his ax, and the rock split in half, revealing Sanshengmu's prison. The mother and the son were reunited.

The Pretty Little Calf

The Pretty Little Calf is another folktale that explores the theme of jealousy.

Once upon a time, there was a man who had three wives. One day, he had to travel away on business, and each of the wives promised to give him something precious upon his return. The first wife promised gold, and the second silver; but the third wife was set on giving him a son. The man was pleased the most with the third wife.

The other two women were jealous. When the man went away and the third wife indeed turned out to be pregnant and, in time, bore a son, they stole him. They wrapped him up in hay and fed him to a buffalo. As the third wife awoke after a torturous delivery, they told her that her child was malformed and died.

Soon, the man came back home. The first and the second wife brought him gold and silver, as promised. But the third wife only had a horrible story of the delivery gone wrong. The man, disappointed, sentenced her to his mill to grind rice there—the hardest type of housework.

But soon, the buffalo who had devoured the child bore a beautiful calf. The man was very fond of it and soon realized that the animal behaved as if it understood human speech. So he set up an experiment: He gave some dumplings to the calf and told it to bring them to its mother.

The calf took the dumplings, as if understanding the command, but it didn't bring them to the buffalo but, instead, to the man's third wife. The man grew slightly suspicious, but he didn't realize the truth—but his first and second wife did. They had to kill the calf.

So they both pretended to be ill. They said that only the calf's liver and skin could cure them. Their husband believed them, but he was too fond of the calf, so he set it free into the woods and killed another one instead.

The calf wandered in the woods until it came to a house of a woman named Huang. The woman was throwing a colorful ball, and the calf caught it on its horn. Huang seemed distressed: She said that she had promised to marry whoever caught the ball, and now she had to marry the calf. A promise was a promise, so she decorated the calf's horns with ribbons to signify the upcoming wedding.

This startled the calf. It ran off, and Huang chased him. She finally arrived at a small pond, where she saw a handsome young man dressed in wedding clothes. She asked him where her calf was. He was the calf, he responded; he had transformed. He told her his whole life story.

Then, the young man and Huang came back to his father's house. The hero exposed his cruel stepmothers but begged his father to show mercy on them. He also restored his mother to her rightful place as his father's wife. He married Huang, and the heroes lived happily ever after.

The Son of a Horse

The Son of a Horse is a folktale told by the Salar people—a Turkic minority in China who live on the northern and southern bank of the Yellow River and are predominantly Muslim. It is only right to include the tale of a minority group who has lived in China for centuries—since at least the 14th century (Dwyer, 2007).

Once upon a time, a family had a beautiful black mare. One day, the mare gave birth to a young boy. The family marveled at this and took the boy to the local imam, or Muslim priest. The imam named the boy Ma Shengbao, which indicated his birth from a horse. The boy grew up as the family's adopted son and became a very distinguished archer and a martial artist.

But Ma Shengbao grew lonely. When he became a young man, he left his house in search of other men who could become his brothers. During his journey, he encountered a tree and a rock from which smoke was coming. He shot his arrows at both of them and found men trapped inside. They soon became his sworn brothers. From that point on, they wandered together.

One day, they met a trio of doves. The doves would temporarily turn into beautiful women in order to prepare a meal for the heroes. Ma Shengbao stole the feathers from the doves' tails and burned them, trapping them in their human bodies forever. The three brothers then married the three maidens, and Ma Shengbao chose the one who was the most beautiful.

After some time of marital bliss, the brothers noticed that their wives were looking pale and thin. They investigated the matter and learned that one day, as the women were looking for the source of fire for their hearth, a demoness followed them home and started preying on them, sucking their blood.

Ma Shengbao set out a trap for the demoness. In the evening, when the monster came to prey on his wife, he hid himself and shot her with his arrow. The demoness ran away, howling in pain, but took Ma's wife with her.

Ma gathered his brothers, and they set out to find the demoness. They came upon a hole in the ground. Ma asked his brothers to lower him inside on a rope. In the hole, he found the demoness and his imprisoned wife. With her help, he killed the monster. After her death, he discovered that the demoness had been hoarding treasure, so he gathered it and sent it up on the rope, along with his wife.

But that was when his brothers betrayed him. They took the treasure and his wife but didn't lower the rope again, leaving Ma stranded in the hole. In vain did the hero look for an alternative way out of the hole; he was stuck. Finally, exhausted, he slept.

When he woke up, he was confronted with an unusual scene: There was a snake and an eagle in the hole, fighting. Ma shot the snake, and the eagle, grateful for the deliverance, offered to take Ma on his back and fly out of the hole.

The eagle left Ma by the well near his house. As the hero rested there, his wife came out to fetch some water. She immediately recognized her husband and clung to him, crying; his brothers were abusing her. Ma, unable to bear this, challenged his brothers to a martial art contest and won. Then, he forced them, along with their wives, to leave their home. He lived there alone with his wife, happy till the end of his days.

The Water Mother

The Water Mother is another example of a tale about a persecuted heroine. It tells a story of a young woman who lived with her cruel mother-in-law. Even though the women could afford to buy water from traders, the mother-in-law insisted that the young woman walk a long way to a well every day and take the water from there. If she failed, she was severely beaten.

One day, once the woman was standing by the well, a thought crossed her mind to drown herself—life was too unbearable. At the same moment, an old woman came up to her. She could, by all accounts, read the girl's thoughts. She told her not to kill herself and gave her a stick. When the girl struck her bucket with the stick, it filled with water on its own. The old woman left her with the stick and with two commandments: never to tell anyone about it and never to strike her bucket twice.

For a time, everything went well. But one day, the cruel mother-in-law found the stick lying by the bucket. It called to her, and it looked like it was more than just an ordinary object. Out of curiosity, the woman struck the bucket twice.

Water started overflowing the bucket. Soon, it couldn't contain it. The water started rising in the house and flowing through the windows. Soon, the whole area was flooded, and both women drowned. Years later, a temple to commemorate this event would be erected in the area, and the young woman with the stick would come to be venerated under the name of the Water Mother.

The Wolf of Zhongshan

The story of the wolf of Zhongshan is set during the time of the Zhou Dynasty, although the characters taking part in it are more mythological than historical (Idema, 2008). Zhongshan was a small warring state during that period.

The king of Zhongshan was riding through a forest. Suddenly, a wolf crossed his path. The king shot his arrow at him but hit a nearby stone instead. The wolf started running, and the king's party followed in pursuit.

As the wolf ran away, he stumbled upon a traveling scholar. The animal begged the scholar for his life. The man, led by the principles of love and compassion that he had been taught, agreed to help the wolf and hid him in his bag. Then, when the hunters approached him, he pretended he didn't know anything about the wolf's whereabouts.

After the king and his men rode away, the wolf jumped out of the scholar's bag. The man wanted to say his goodbyes, but the animal stopped him. He begged the scholar to save his life again because he was starving. The scholar then offered him a pie, but the wolf refused. This was no proper meal for an animal like him. The man offered his donkey, but still, the wolf refused. Only human flesh would satisfy him, he said.

The scholar cried out in anguish. He accused the wolf of being ungrateful for the help he had been given. But the wolf only shrugged: His life hadn't been really saved, had it? He was starving now, and he would die if he didn't eat the man before him, so the act of saving his life would only be complete then.

Soon, a fight for the wolf's life turned into a veritable philosophical debate. They couldn't solve it, however, so they had to present their case to a council of three elders.

The first elder turned out to be an old apricot tree. It sided with the wolf: It had been used to giving fruit all its life, and now it was about to be chopped into wood. Only by losing its own life would the tree have helped the people around it, it said.

The second elder was an old buffalo. It also sided with the wolf: It had provided milk for its master and now it was about to be butchered, thus completing its act of sacrifice.

The wolf was overjoyed, thinking that he had already won the argument. But there was still the third elder to consult: an old farmer. The man heard the whole story and nodded sagely. He said he understood the wolf; however, he had one problem with the tale. It was difficult for him to believe that the wolf could have fit into the scholar's bag in the first place. The wolf, indignant, crawled into the bag again in order to demonstrate that what he'd said was true.

That was when the farmer tied the bag securely and started beating the wolf. He battered him but didn't kill him. When he finally untied the bag, the image the wolf presented was truly pitiful, and the scholar felt bad for him. But at that same time, the farmer's wife entered the scene. She said that not a few days' prior, the wolf had eaten their little son.

That was when the scholar lost all compassion. He landed a fatal blow on the wolf's head, killing it. Thus, a pseudo-philosophical debate ended with retribution.

Ye Xian

Our last story in this collection is another Cinderella-type tale, very similar to the *Beauty and Pock Face*. But this time, the tale of two daughters, one of whom, Ye

Xian, was persecuted, is set in a semi-historical, semi-legendary community of cave dwellers from before the Han Dynasty. Another difference is that the spirit of the heroine's dead mother came back not in the form of a cow but as a fish, to whom the girl confided her struggles.

The fish was then killed by the cruel stepmother and served for dinner, but Ye Xian buried its bones in a pot. In the place where she did so, her mother's spirit would linger, and when the time came to go to the New Year's celebrations and Ye Xian was banned from doing so, her mother gave her a lavish dress and special slippers to wear for the occasion.

From there, the tale follows a pattern that is more familiar to anyone acquainted with the Cinderella story: Ye Xian went to the New Year's feast and was admired by everyone, but she had to run away because she was afraid her family would recognize her. She lost one of her slippers as she did.

The slipper was then found by a peasant passing the road home. As it was very precious, he traded it to a local merchant, who then sold it further. The shoe went through several hands, until it found its way to the local king, who was amazed by its small size. The king was determined to find the owner of the shoe.

Ye Xian, seeing advertisements hanging everywhere, went to the palace to claim her shoe. But because she was wearing her everyday tattered dress, she was mistaken for a thief. Guards seized her and brought her before the king, who, being a just monarch, wanted to listen to her side of the story before passing the verdict.

He was immediately struck by the girl's beauty and kindness, and he believed her words. The next day, he went up to her home and, to her stepmother's chagrin and jealousy, he took Ye Xian as his bride.

Conclusion

We have reached the end of our journey. By now, you have probably realized that the rich world of Chinese myth and folklore, with not hundreds, but thousands of years of tradition, simply cannot be contained within the confines of one book. Hence, let this conclusion serve as an encouragement: to explore more stories, characters, and creatures from that rich tradition. It is my hope, however, that this book provided you with a good foundation for further studies, that you now better understand the various traditions that formed the Chinese folk religion with its mythology and philosophy, and that you have a wider knowledge of stories found in Chinese novels, oral folktales, and poetic inscriptions. Let this book become a guide on your continuing journey through the fascinating Chinese civilization and culture.

References

Adcock, W. (2003). *I Ching*. Hermes House.

Adler, J. (2005). Chinese religion: An overview. In L. Jones (Ed.), *Encyclopedia of religion, 2nd edition*. Macmillan Reference USA.

Adler, J. (2020). Confucianism as a religious tradition: Linguistic and methodological problems. *Confucianism in dialogue with cultures and religions: A conference in honor of Professor Tu Weiming*.

Allen, R. (2019). *Shouxing—the Chinese god of old age (Chinese mythology)*. Godchecker. https://www.godchecker.com/chinese-mythology/SHOUXING/

Beauchamp, F. (2010). Asian origins of Cinderella: The Zhuang storyteller of Guangxi. *Oral Tradition, 25*(2). https://doi.org/10.1353/ort.2010.0023

Birrell, A. (1999). *Chinese mythology: An introduction*. Johns Hopkins University Press.

Brown, J., & Brown, J. (2006). *China, Japan, Korea: Culture and customs*. Booksurge.

Burham, H. (2015). *The esoteric codex: Deities of knowledge*. LULU Press.

Cahill, S. E. (2013). Sublimation in medieval China: The case of the mysterious woman of the nine heavens. *Journal of Chinese Religions*, *20*(1), 91–102. https://doi.org/10.1179/073776992805307692

Caishen: Chinese deity. (2019). Encyclopedia Britannica. https://www.britannica.com/topic/Caishen

Chamberlain, J., & Eaton, J. (2014). *Chinese gods: An introduction to Chinese folk religion.* Blacksmith Books.

Chang, R. H. (2000). Understanding Di and Tian: Deity and Heaven from Shang to Tang Dynasties. *Sino-Platonic Papers*, *108*.

Ch'eng, M. (1995). *The origin of Chinese deities.* Foreign Languages Press.

Christie, A. (1968). *Chinese mythology.* Hamlyn House.

Clark, H. R. (2007). *Portrait of a community: Society, culture, and the structures of kinship in the Mulan River Valley (Fujian) from the Late Tang through the Song.* Chinese University Press.

Cullen, C. (2008). Cosmogony: Overview. In *The encyclopedia of Taoism* (pp. 47–48). Routledge.

Do-Dinh, P. (1969). *Confucius and Chinese humanism.* Funk & Wagnalls.

Dwyer, A. M. (2007). *Salar: A study in inner Asian language contact processes.* Otto Harrassowitz Verlag.

Eberhard, W. (2015). *Dictionary of Chinese symbols: Hidden symbols in Chinese life and thought.* Routledge.

Eberhard, W. (1965). *Folktales of China.* University of Chicago Press.

Ebrey, P. B., & Walthall, A. (2014). *East Asia: A cultural, social, and political history.* Cengage Learning.

Eskildsen, S. (2012). *The teachings and practices of the early Quanzhen Taoist masters.* State University of New York Press.

Forke, A. (1925). *The world-conception of the Chinese.* Probsthain.

4 Chinese ghost stories you should know. (2015). Projectpengyou.org. https://projectpengyou.org/4-chinese-ghost-stories-you-should-know/

Fowler, J. D. (2005). *An introduction to the philosophy and religion of Taoism: Pathways to immortality.* Sussex Academic Press.

Geertz, A. W., Mccutcheon, R. T., & Elliott, S. S. (2000). *Perspectives on method and theory in the study of religion: Adjunct proceedings of the XVIIth Congress of the International Association for the History of Religions, Mexico City, 1995.* Brill.

Girardot, N. J. (1976). The problem of creation mythology in the study of Chinese religion. *History of Religions, 15*(4), 289–318. https://doi.org/10.1086/462748

Gold, M. (2015, January 19). *Taiwan's gays pray for soul mates at "Rabbit" temple.* Reuters. https://www.reuters.com/article/taiwan-gay-temple-idINKBN0KS0R120150119

Hawkes, D. (1968). *The songs of the South.* Penguin.

Huang, M. W. (2006). Reconstructing Haohan in three novels from the Sui-Tang romance cycle. In *Negotiating masculinities in Late Imperial China.* University of Hawaii Press.

Hucker, C. O. (2008). *China's imperial past: An introduction to Chinese history and culture.* Stanford University Press.

Idema, W. L. (2008). *Personal salvation and filial piety: Two precious scroll narratives of Guanyin and her acolytes.* University Of Hawai'i Press.

Kang, X. (2006). *The cult of the fox: Power, gender, and popular religion in late imperial and modern China.* Columbia University Press.

Karlgren, B. (1946). Legends and cults in Ancient China. *Bulletin of the Museum of Far Eastern Antiquities, 18*(261).

Lagerwey, J., & Kalinowski, M. (2009). *Early Chinese religion, part one: Shang through Han (1250 BC-220 AD)*. Brill.

Lama Lodu. (2011). *Bardo teachings*. Shambhala Publications.

Lang, G. (2011). *Social scientific studies of religion in China: Methodology, theories, and findings*. Brill. https://brill.com/view/title/18128

Lee, A. C. C. (2005). *God's Asian names: Rendering the biblical God in Chinese*. Www.sbl-Site.org. https://www.sbl-site.org/publications/article.aspx?articleId=456

Lee, Y. K. (2002). Building the chronology of early Chinese history. *Asian Perspectives*, *41*(1), 15–42. https://doi.org/10.1353/asi.2002.0006

Li Gu o Lin. (n.d.). *Encyclopedia of Chinese pantheon*. Scribd. Retrieved April 12, 2023, from https://www.scribd.com/document/270981438/Encyclopedia-of-Chinese-Pantheon#

Liu, W. G. (2015). *The Chinese market economy, 1000-1500*. State University Of New York Press.

Liu, P. (2016). "Conceal my body so that I can protect the state": The making of the mysterious woman in Daoism and water margin. *Ming Studies*, *2016*(74), 48–71. https://doi.org/10.1080/0147037x.2016.1228876

Liu, A., & Major, J. S. (2010). *The Huainanzi: A guide to the theory and practice of government in early Han China.* Columbia University Press.

Mair, V. H. (2012). *Tao Te Ching: The classic book of integrity and the Way.* Random House Publishing Group.

Modelski, G. (2000). *World cities: -3000 to 2000.* Faros.

Ni, X. C. (2018). *The long list of Chinese ghost stories and ghoulish creatures.* Https://Radii.co. https://radii.co/article/long-list-chinese-ghost-stories

Perkins, D. (1999). *Encyclopedia of China: The essential reference to China, its history and culture.* Fitzroy Dearborn.

Pregadio, F. (2008). *Encyclopedia of Taoism.* Routledge.

Qilin: Definition & facts. (1998). In *Encyclopedia Britannica.* https://www.britannica.com/topic/qilin

Roberts, J. (2010). *Chinese mythology: A to Z.* Chelsea House.

Shahar, M., & Weller, R. P. (1996). *Unruly gods: Divinity and society in China.* University Of Hawai'i Press.

Slingerland, E. G. (2003). *Effortless action: Wu-wei as conceptual metaphor and spiritual ideal in early China.* Oxford University Press.

Stepanchuk, C., & Choy, C. (1991). *Mooncakes and hungry ghosts: Festivals of China*. China Books & Periodicals.

Szonyi, M. (1998). The cult of Hu Tianbao and the eighteenth-century discourse of homosexuality. *Late Imperial China*, *19*(1), 1–25. https://doi.org/10.1353/late.1998.0004

Taagepera, R. (1997). Expansion and contraction patterns of large polities: Context for Russia. *International Studies Quarterly*, *41*(3), 475–504. https://doi.org/10.1111/0020-8833.00053

Teiser, S. F. (1996). *The ghost festival in medieval China*. Princeton University Press.

Teiser, S. T. (1995). Popular religion. *Journal of Asian Studies*, *54*(2), 378–395. https://doi.org/10.2307/2058743

Theobald, U. (2018). *Sheji 社稷, the state altars of soil and grain*. China Knowledge.http://www.chinaknowledge.de/History/Terms/sheji.html

Twitchett, D. C., & Fairbank, J. K. (1978). *The Cambridge history of China*. Cambridge University Press.

Unschuld, P. U. (1986). *Medicine in China: A history of pharmaceutics*. University of California Press.

Unschuld, P. U., Tessenow, H., & Zheng, J. (2011). *Huang di nei jing su wen: An annotated translation of*

Huang Di's inner classic—basic questions. University of California Press.

Valentino, B. A. (2005). *Final solutions: Mass killing and genocide in the twentieth century.* Cornell University Press.

Wang, D. (2008). *China's unequal treaties: Narrating national history.* Lexington Books.

Wolf, A. P., & Martin, E. (1978). *Studies in Chinese society.* Stanford University Press.

Wu, C. (1982). *The Chinese heritage.* Crown Publishers, Inc.

Wu, C., & Yu, A. C. (2012). *The journey to the West.* The University of Chicago Press.

Xu, Y. (2002). *Ancient Chinese writing: Oracle bone inscriptions from the ruins of Yin.* Academia Sinica. National Palace Museum.

Yan, H.-S. (2010). *Reconstruction designs of lost ancient Chinese machinery.* Springer.

Yang, C. K. (1961). *Religion in Chinese society: A study of contemporary social functions of religion and some of their historical factors.* University of California Press.

Yang, L., An, D., & Turner, J. A. (2008). *Handbook of Chinese mythology.* Oxford University Press.

Yao, X., & Zhao, Y. (2010). *Chinese religion: A contextual approach*. Continuum.

Yu, Y. I., & Branscum, J. Y. (2021). *The shadow book of Ji Yun: The Chinese classic of weird true tales, horror stories, and occult knowledge*. Empress Wu Books.

Yuan, H. (2006). *The magic lotus lantern and other tales from the Han Chinese*. Westport, Conn. Libraries Unlimited.

Yuan, H. (2008). *Princess Peacock: Tales from the other peoples of China*. Libraries Unlimited.

Zhelyazkov, Y. (2022, January 19). *Shouxing (Shalou)— Chinese god of longevity*. Symbol Sage. https://symbolsage.com/chinese-god-of-longevity/

Made in the USA
Monee, IL
21 November 2023

47082958R00092